Kingdom Deployment:
Operating In Your Created Design For Your Eternal Purpose

Charlie Lewis

The Kingdom System Series

Volume III

Kingdom Media

Kingdom Deployment: Operating In Your Created Design For Your Eternal Purpose
The Kingdom System Series
by Charlie Lewis

Printed in the United States of America

ISBN: 978-0-9965900-2-0

www.kindgdommedia.info

Foundational Statement

This is the third book in the three book series about the Kingdom System; Kingdom Deployment - Operating In Your Created Design For Your Eternal Purpose. As we have done in the first two books, we will present a positional statement of understanding for the materials that are being presented.

Why is this necessary? Our faith has been hijacked and made religious. Faith is not religious, it is relational. When most of humanity sees anything about God, our Creator, God's recorded word, the church, believers or anything that involves Faith or Belief, they automatically turn off, tune it out and want nothing to do with the information. Reality is very different than our perception. This book presents a relationship of great faith that is not based on religious concepts or religious beliefs. This information is about a living vibrant relationship and how to develop and to maintain such a relationship.

1) This is not a religious book nor is this a book about religion.

2) Our God is not a religious God. He is the God of relationship.

3) God's Word is not about religion. It is about relationship. From cover to cover there is the presentation of how to be in a vibrant, living relationship with the true and the living God.

4) God's Word is about Kingdom. From the beginning to the last recorded words, the reality of our experience "in-time," on planet earth the reality of Kingdom can be seen everywhere. The truth is presented that on our planet there are A) two Kingdoms, B) one King, C) one who wants to be King, and D) there is an epic battle raging for the lives of humanity.

5) In the first book the Kingdom series, *The Kingdom System - A Pattern for Guaranteed Success*, the presentation of the facts about how our God works with and through humanity by the means of a system was presented.
Everything that our God created operates within a system. He continues this method of systems with humanity. He provides the plan for success for all of humanity through the system that he has provided. That system is called the Kingdom of God. That system is operable and fully functional on the earth presently. God Himself as Jesus Christ brought the system to the earth and delivered it to humanity so that all of humanity can be successful. **The System is not religious.** This information that was presented in the *Kingdom System* uncovers the facts about the existance of the System and knowing these facts is where **knowledge** begins for humanity to operate successfully on earth. But just knowing the facts is not enough.

6) In the second book in the Kingdom series, *Kingdomnomics the Dynamics of Conduct and Behavior,* we discussed how the facts about the Kingdom System relate to each of us personally. We explore how we engage this system in our personal lives and how we make this knowledge a part of the daily living of our lives? We found that the teaching of values and principles is more than information just about laws involving regulation and compliance. Often with the laws of man, we believe that we can get away with not obeying them **without consequence** if no one sees us or if we do not get caught. Dynamics are different. Dynamics operate by design. They produce their results and their outcomes because of the way that they are designed and we cannot escape their predetermined outcomes. They are part of an interactive system of competing or conflicting forces that are activated by our choice of action. Gravity is an example of a dynamic. Forgiveness and Morality are also dynamics.
   Knowing the facts **(knowledge)** and then knowing how to make that knowledge work personally for each of us is **considered to be wisdom** for humanity.
7) In this third book of the Kingdom series, *Kingdom Deployment – Operating in Your Created Design for Your Eternal Purpose,* we will explore how the **facts** that we have gained become the **knowledge** that we use to make the personal application of our facts to our lives and that then becomes wisdom for us. When we **understand** how all of this fits into our Creator's plan

for all of humanity this completes the relationship cycle of knowledge, wisdom and understanding.

Our Creator's plan for humanity is completely about the individual, but it is never just about the individual. His plan always includes all of humanity. This study is amazing. We learn about eternity; about our created design for our eternal purpose. We discover the difference between Employment and Deployment, and between Income and Outcome. Our relationship with our Creator escalates to a new level of relationship through the reality and the understanding of this process. The knowledge (facts) have become personal (wisdom) for us and we see clearly how all of this fits into our Creator's plan for all of humanity (understanding). We are ready to begin the journey of developing our effectiveness in the Kingdom and enhancing our understanding of our God, His Kingdom System, how the system works through *Kingdomnomics – Dynamics of Conduct and Behavior,* and then Deploying the Kingdom System into our societies to impact our culture for the glory of our God and for the betterment of all of humanity.

TABLE OF CONTENTS

Foundational Statement....................iv

Introduction xi

Chapter 1: The Shaping of Culture 20

Chapter 2: Eternity The Perspective and Vantage Point....................27

Chapter 3: What is "Created Design"?....................37

Chapter 4: Understanding Eternal Purpose 47

Chapter 5: The Investment Dynamic....................57

Chapter 6: Is Eternity Our Option and/or Our Choice? 66

Chapter 7: The Necessity of Purpose 90

Chapter 8: The Loss and Absence of Hope....................102

Summary and Conclusion....................115

Personal Confessions.................... 133

A. Exodus 28

B. Spirit, Mind, Body

C. Commitment For The Word

Introduction

In the first two books in *The Kingdom System Series* we have advanced our study to the place where we must now take a look at the big or bigger picture of the System's Influence on our personal lives and the influence in the lives of those around us. We have followed the pattern that we have established in all of our studies. We begin with the knowledge or the facts. We then determine how those facts apply to each of us personally and we believe that these results become wisdom for us. When we know the facts and how those facts apply to us personally, we now must explore how the knowledge and the wisdom that we have researched and determined to be correct fits into our Creator's plan for all of humanity – (both the present and the future influences.) We call this understanding.

In *The Kingdom System, A Pattern for Guaranteed Success* we began by asking if our life experiences were reflective and representative of the experiences that are described in the Great Book of Learning for those who are people of faith. Our lives are described as powerful lives of dominion and authority with overcoming victory. We are told that we are more than conquerors. We are told that in every situation we are made to triumph in and through Christ Jesus who is our redeemer and the one who restores us to a life of victory and success. We are described as treading upon serpents and scorpions and as having authority and power over all of the power of the enemy.

We do not live insulated lives in glass domes. We are not exempt from the situations, the circumstances and the relationships that are often developed because of our decisions or choices of action. The unfavorable results are used by our enemy, the defeated Satan to test our relationship with our Creator and our faithful God. We must first know that we are provided with the Kingdom System, and this System is the method for our victory. Someone said that there is no testimony without a test. There is no victory without a battle. But we are not pawns. We are not victims. We must know that where we are is no surprise to our God. We must also know that He has made provision for every need that we will ever encounter long before the need ever became evident to us.

God Himself as Jesus Christ came to the earth and He delivered the System for our success to all of humanity. Not just for a few or even just for the religious, but for all of humanity. It is His will that none should perish, but that "everyone" should have everlasting life. Who is not included in the description "everyone"?

In the Book of Kingdoms in the presentation about the shrewd servant the young rabbi Jesus told His disciples that the people of the Kingdom of Darkness know how to use their System for their benefit better than those of His kingdom know how to use the System that He has provided to them for their benefit. Sadly today most people of faith do not know that there is a System that is provided to them for their successful operation on the earth.

This system was the central and the primary theme and the dominating message of all of the teaching of Christ when He was on the earth. It is presented as the Government of Heaven and it includes access to all of Heaven's resources including (the Angel Armies of God). This System is available through the currency of faith to all Believers. We are told that the System rules over everything. We are encouraged to call all of the power and all of the authority of the Government of Heaven to the earth to intervene in our situations, in our circumstances and in our relationships. This produces much glory (a good reputation) for our King and for our God. This is made available for the benefit of the people of faith as well as for the benefit of all of humanity who understands the provision, those who accept and believe in the provision and those who then apply the appropriate dynamics in their decision making process.

In the book *Kingdomnomics, The Dynamics of Conduct and Behavior,* we discovered that dynamics operate by design. There is no human influence in the functioning or in the outcomes of dynamics. Laws are often about regulation and compliance. There is usually an appointed judge who decides the acceptability of our performance based on their interpretation and on an arbitrary standard that has been established by other humans. That is not how the Kingdom System operates. These dynamics and their predetermined outcomes follow the course of our chosen actions whether we are aware of their existence and their influence or even if we are not. They are active and their influence and their impact is not diminished by our lack of knowledge or by our lack of understanding of their principles. Ignorance is no excuse. They function by their created design. Gravity, inertia and all of the other systems of the world do not depend on our awareness or upon our understanding for their successful operation and for their designed outcomes. It is our knowledge and our understanding of their designed principles that allows us to direct the outcomes for our good by our chosen actions. **Our choice of action is the stimulus that activates the inertia contained in our selected action towards their inherent results.**

With this knowledge and with our knowing the facts, we can act with wisdom. When we know how these facts impact and apply to us personally, we **can choose** our outcomes. We actually **do choose** always, in every situation. **We choose** our outcomes by our chosen decisions of action. We can choose success. Every time in every situation, in every circumstance and in each relationship. We can select and we can make the correct choices for the outcomes that we choose to experience and that we want to enjoy and that align with our desired outcomes.

Does this sound too simple? The ways of our Creator and our God are not complicated nor are they too difficult to understand. They are always simple and they are always easy to understand. It is our enemy, the defeated Satan, the one who wants to be king who distorts the questions and then uses deceit to create confusion and doubt in our minds. "Did he really say that? You will become like God? He does not want you to know nor to understand. God is too hard. He requires more than we can deliver. His love is conditional. You have to earn His love."

When we only know about Him, it is easy to be convinced of anything about him. It is through relationship that faith is developed. Faith without relationship is really not faith at all. It is more appropriately described as religion. Relationship requires that we spend time together with our God. How do we do this? We begin to fellowship with Him by reading His Word and by training and by teaching our spirits to communicate directly with His Spirit. We are charged to reprogram our minds by His Word. When we do, we will think as He thinks and we simply develop the habit where we allocate time to be with Him. Through the fellowship of our spirit to His Spirit and from our mind to His mind, our relationship becomes established through the communication that only can be achieved by spirit to spirit and mind to mind fellowship. Our thoughts become agreeable with His will, and our plans succeed.

If we do not know about the Kingdom System, the plan and the method that our Creator has provided for our success we experience frustration. When we become aware of the System and when we do the research to learn about the interactive System of Dynamics that provides the understanding of the choices that we are available for us to engage in order to direct and to guarantee our chosen outcomes for success, we have the facts and we know how to apply those facts personally for good outcomes in our life experiences.

Where the Kingdom System and the Kingdomnomic Dynamics are about our knowing personally how to engage the

System for our benefit and for our success, The Kingdom is also very much about community. The plan and the design of the Kingdom system are not for anyone's selfish or self-centered gain. The Kingdom is about all of Humanity and all of the instruction and the discipline contained therein are provided for the good and for the proper respect of everyone. Kingdom is about culture. A Kingdom culture is an inclusive culture of an extensively defined and completely easy to understand plan of Kingdom with a common community culture as its objective. The Kingdom is a "common unity" approach. Everyone is working for the common good of everyone.

In the study and in the presentation of the Kingdom System as the System provided by our Creator God and the King of our Kingdom, understanding that there is a System provided for our success is the first step in a three step process for the successful understanding and for the effective engagement in the provisions of our System. Second in the process was the presentation of the Kingdomnomic Dynamics of Conduct and Behavior as the method of how we engage and how we employ the System in our lives for our success. The third and very clear next step is the understanding of Kingdom Deployment. All three presentations are necessary for the correct understanding and for the effective engagement of the Kingdom System in the lives of humanity.

Understanding and engaging Kingdom Deployment is exciting. Humanity is desperately searching for the Kingdom and for its understanding.

The Systems of this world are not working. In every sphere of influence they are failing;

Governments are failing. They have become more about themselves rather than about those they represent. They pass laws and enforce them on their citizens and exempt themselves from the same laws. I believe that is called tyranny not representation.

Economies everywhere are in trouble. Currency is greatly devalued and spending is out of control. It is challenging to get ahead and to stay ahead of the growth curve with money. Savings and planning is at an all time low. Someone said "the more you make, the more it takes." The system eats up everything you make. Taxes are outrageous and inflation is out of control.

Media is corrupt and biased. There is very little that is trustworthy that comes from media. Whether your source is conservative or liberal, they all seem to have a personal agenda.

The **Family** as presented in the book of Kingdoms is under attack. The attack is violent. It is not subtle. If you do not agree with their corrupt and distorted philosophy, you too become a target of their assault. The family is foundational in the Kingdom System. It is the relational building block on which everything else is built. The function and the make-up of a family are not difficult to understand.

Education has become so manipulated by people with special interests that everything is for their good and for their self-preservation. The mission of education for the good of students appears to have been lost. History is being rewritten to reflect an inaccurate liberal agenda. What began as an institutions of faith to teach values and principles have become bastions of ridicule for anything including faith in our Creator.

The **Arts and Entertainment** have become very common and extremely vulgar. If it isn't sex or witches, or evil spirits and murder, it probably will not make it in Hollywood. The beauty of the inspiration and the talent that comes from our Creator has been replaced with murder and mayhem.

Religion has become a huge industry with most of its effort directed towards self-preservation. Religion is big business. The revenues generated from religious organizations would rival those from government, the oil companies, insurance companies and the banking industry. Very little of the revenues from religious activities make it to those in need. Most of the revenue goes to support the staff and the plant for the operation. Most programs minister to those who are already there.

The Kingdom System, Kingdomnomics and the Dynamics of conduct and Behavior and then the Deployment into the cultural centers of influence as Ambassadors of the Good News of the Gospel of the Kingdom will change society into a Kingdom Society where a new day of goodness and success will dawn on the earth. The Kingdom System is **the correct choice to the alternative systems of the world.** For success the Kingdom System must become dominate relationally and experientially for all of humanity as their primary operating system on the earth.

We will delve into the Kingdom Deployment and all of its impact and influence on the cultures of humanity.

Chapter 1

The Shaping of Culture

Proverbs 2:2–12 (New Living Translation)

2 Tune your ears to wisdom, and concentrate on understanding.

3 Cry out for insight, and ask for understanding.

4 Search for them as you would for silver; seek them like hidden treasures.

5 Then you will understand what it means to fear the Lord, and you will gain knowledge of God.

6 For the Lord grants wisdom! From his mouth come knowledge and understanding.

7 He grants a treasure of common sense to the honest. He is a shield to those who walk with integrity.

8 He guards the paths of the just and protects those who are faithful to him.

9 Then you will understand what is right, just, and fair, and you will find the right way to go.

10 For wisdom will enter your heart, and knowledge will fill you with joy.

11 Wise choices will watch over you. Understanding will keep you safe.

12 Wisdom will save you from evil people, from those whose words are twisted.

Knowledge is knowing the facts. Wisdom is knowing how the facts apply to you personally. Understanding is when you know how all of your knowledge and your wisdom relate to and fit into the Creator's master plan for all of humanity.

There appears to be an evident misunderstanding and often a significant and debilitating disconnect between humanity's understanding of their individual purpose and of their created design in their choice of acts, actions and decisions while on earth. In our most inner man, our spirit, we know that much is missing from the resulting experiences of the choices that we are taught to make. How are we taught? From where do we learn?

We will explore at a later time the sources of our learning. They are many and varied.

We will begin this research by looking at several pertinent definitions. If we ask incorrect questions and if we are seeking incorrect goals, we will arrive at an incorrect place with an incorrect understanding. Our destination is important in eternity. We must operate our lives asking the correct questions and going after the correct goals. We must seek the goals that align with our created design for our given eternal purpose.

Let's investigate the following simple words and their definitions. Perhaps they will add light to our understanding.

This is an exciting exercise. It will add clarity, understanding and direction to our living.

Definitions

1) **Employment**
   A. **The activity and/or occupation that we perform in order to receive revenue for our livelihood.**
   B. **The condition or position of receiving pay for our work.**

2) **Deployment**
   A. **To bring forces or materials or people into action.**
   B. **To organize and to send out people or things to be used for a particular purpose.**
   C. **The methodical procedure of introducing an activity, a process, a program or a system to all applicable areas of an operation.**

3) **Income**
   A. **What we receive for our work.**

4) **Outcome**
   A. **The way a thing turns out.**
   B. **The consequence or results of our actions.**
   C. **What we become.**

5) <u>Eternal/Eternity</u>

A. Having no beginning or end in time.
B. Lasting forever.
C. Always existing.
D. Always true or valid.

6) <u>Temporal/Temporary</u>

A. Of or relating to time as opposed to eternity.
B. Secular.
C. Worldly as opposed to spiritual.

7) <u>Life</u>

A. Acts, actions and decisions that generate positive growth, positive change and/or improvement in your relationship with your Creator. Choices that assist in the fulfillment and in the achievement of your created design and in the accomplishment of your eternal purpose.

B. Acts, actions and decisions that enhance the outcomes of your living and your life experience.

8) <u>Death</u>

A. Acts, actions and decisions that generate negative growth, negative change and/or result in separation in your relationship with your Creator. Choices that direct you away from the fulfillment and the achievement of your created design and your eternal purpose.

B. Acts, actions and decisions that defeat and destroy the positive outcomes of your living and your life experience.

9) <u>Light</u>

A. The natural agent that stimulates sight and makes things visible.

B. Understanding of a problem or mystery.

C. Enlightenment.

10) <u>Darkness</u>

A. The partial or total absence of light.

B. Wickedness or evil.

11) <u>Plan</u>

A. A detailed proposal for doing or achieving something.

B. A detailed diagram, drawing, program or system in particular.

12) <u>Purpose</u>

A. The reason for which someone or something is created.

B. The reason for which someone or something exists.

C. The reason for which something is done.

D. An intended or desired result.

E. The end, the aim, the goal.

<u>Please refer back to these definitions as needed in our study and in the review of our deployment into our created design for our eternal purpose.</u>

Our culture is the result of what we believe and the way that we think. Culture is determined on many levels of relationship: individually, as a family, as a community, as a society, as a nation and as people. The way we think in our culture is influenced by many things: our environment, our observations, what we are taught and what we experience personally. Our culture is constantly changing. During our lifetime we discover that how we view many important understandings will change as our life experiences change. For example, we will see truth, morality, integrity, faithfulness, generosity, benevolence, success and many other subjects from different vantage points. A child who is five years old sees things very differently than a woman who is twenty-five years old or a man who is fifty-five years of age. This is not a surprise nor is it unexpected.

Many factors contribute to this experience, and all can be described as the observation from differing vantage points. A vantage point is the place or location from which a person is observing a matter. That place can differ greatly depending on many factors. Among these factors are education, environment, experience and one's position in life. These factors alone provide valid and accurate input from which to observe, review and evaluate a matter.

Much of what is used to determine value and to establish correctness in our world is determined from wherever we find our present vantage point. While this may be an accurate assessment, additional factors must be considered. For complete accuracy it is necessary to have a reference that is stable; it does not change; the reference is steadfast, sure and eternal; it is one upon which we can and must trust for the conduct of our lives. This conduct is based on our belief and on our acceptance of the stability and the reliability of these provisions—provisions we know are provided for our benefit.

An eternal reference always relies on a vertical orientation more than it does on the horizontal perspective. Our reference for accuracy must be from both the horizontal vantage point, and our reference must also include a viewpoint from the eternal and the vertical vantage point of an authority that is greater than we ourselves are.

Sadly, the vertical which guides our actions from the eternal reference is often not included in our consideration. It is interesting that when a vertical reference is included, we have a relationship and a solution based on the union of a horizontal plank and a vertical plank. Where this union forms a cross creates the strongest point in the union of the two planks. This junction of the two planks is called the nexus, the place where the two planks come together. Is this ironic or coincidental, or does this provide a reference or vantage point proving that where the horizontal and the vertical come together, the planks are strongest? Our vision and our focus are strongest when we include a vertical and eternal reference to our horizontal understanding.

Chapter Two

Eternity As a Perspective and Vantage Point

> ***Ecclesiastes 3:11 (based on Amplified)***
> ***He has made everything beautiful in its time. He also has planted eternity in men's hearts and in men's minds for [a divinely implanted sense of a purpose working through the ages (the generations of time) which nothing under the sun but God alone can satisfy].***
> ***(Personal Paraphrase)***

Eternity and things that are eternal are defined as:

1) Having no beginning nor an end in time;

2) Lasting forever;

3) Always existing; and

4) Always true and/or valid.

Please refer back to this definition as needed in our study and review.

In the process of the living of our lives, our daily routine does not include a great amount of thought or consideration from the perspective of eternity. We appear to be consumed with the activity of the here and now and with the challenges of making today work. After all, eternity is out there somewhere in our futures, way ahead of us when we die. While we may have a fundamental awareness of the existence or the presence of eternity, we believe that we have plenty of time to consider the impact and the outcomes of eternity on our daily lives at a later date. Many believe that eternity begins when we die.

Man's attempt to explain eternity through religion has fostered the belief that eternity is something that is not important now. If eternity is to be considered at all, it is to be considered in our future. That is where and when there is impact for humanity: in our future and not now.

This appears to follow the same thought process where humanity has been taught to consider employment, and gives little or no important thought or sustained consideration to deployment. **Employment has to do with our income (temporary), and our deployment addresses our outcome (eternity).**

In the Great Book of Learning or the Book of Kingdoms, eternity and the things that are eternal are a predominant theme. **In the King James Version, the words eternal or eternity are used 48 times in 48 verses. In the New Living Translation, *eternal* or *eternity* are used 122 times in 117 verses. Few subjects have that many references.** Most of the major doctrines of the Church are not even close. Yet not much is taught about the subject of eternity other than as a consideration in the preparation for dying.

The understanding and the application of eternity are so much more than just as a preparation for dying. To miss the full understanding and the enormous benefit of the application of eternity in our lives and in our daily living is to miss our deepest meaning and the very purpose of our lives.

Mark addresses both the experience of being "in-time" and of being "in eternity." Clearly both provide impact in benefit and in relationship in the life experience of believers and of the followers of Jesus.

> **Mark 10:30 – King James Version** – But he shall receive an hundredfold (**now in this time**), houses, and brethren, and sisters, and mothers, and children, and lands with persecutions: and (**in the world to come eternal life**).

The most important things in our lives are eternal. Let's look at a few.

1. Our spirit is eternal –

Ecclesiastes 12:7 – New Living Translation – Then the dust will return to the earth, and **the spirit will return to God** who gave it.

Luke 23:46 – New Living Translation – Then Jesus shouted, **"Father, I entrust my spirit into your hands."** And with those words, he breathed his last breath.

Acts 7:59 – New Living Translation – As they stoned him, Stephen prayed, **"Lord Jesus, receive my spirit."**

2 Corinthians 5:1 – New Living Translation – For we know that when this earthly tent we live in is taken down (that is, when we die and leave this earthly body) we **will have a house in heaven,** an **eternal body made for us by God himself** and not by human hands.

2. Our Creator/God is eternal –

Genesis 21:33 – New Living Translation – he worshiped the Lord, the **Eternal God.**

Deuteronomy 33:27 – New Living Translation – **The eternal God** is your refuge and His everlasting arms are under you.

Isaiah 26:4 – New Living Translation – for **the Lord is the eternal rock.**

Isaiah 43:13 – New Living Translation – from **eternity to eternity I am God.**

Romans 9:5 – New Living Translation – as the prophets foretold and as the **Eternal God** has commanded.

1 John 5:20 – New Living Translation – **He is the only true God, and He is Eternal Life.**

3. The Kingdom System of Government from our God is eternal –

Daniel 7:14 – New Living Translation – **His rule is Eternal** – it will never end. His Kingdom will never be destroyed.

[2] **Peter 1:11 – New Living Translation** – Then God will give you a grand entrance into the **Eternal Kingdom of our Lord** and Savior Jesus Christ.

Daniel 2:44 – New Living Translation – The God of Heaven will set up **a kingdom that will never be destroyed or conquered. It will** crush all of these kingdoms into nothingness, and it **will stand forever.**

4. The Word of our God is eternal –

Psalms 119:89 – New International Version – Your **word, Lord, is eternal;** it stands firm in the heavens.

[1] **Peter 1:25 – New Living Translation** – But the **word of the Lord remains forever.**

Isaiah 40:8 – New Living Translation – The grass withers and the flowers fade, but the **word of our God stands forever.**

5. God's Love and his mercy are forever eternal – Psalm 136 1–5 – New Living Translation

1 Give thanks to the LORD, for he is good! **His faithful love endures forever.**

2 Give thanks to the God of gods. **His faithful love endures forever.**

3 Give thanks to the Lord of lords. **His faithful love endures forever.**

4 Give thanks to him who alone does mighty miracles. **His faithful love endures forever.**

5 Give thanks to him who made the heavens so skillfully. **His faithful love endures forever.**
(Continues through verse 26)

Jeremiah 31:3 – New Living Translation – [3] Long ago the LORD said to Israel: **"I have loved you, my people, with an everlasting love. With unfailing love** I have drawn you to myself.

Psalm 103:17 – King James Version – [17] **But the mercy of the LORD is from everlasting** to everlasting upon them that fear him, and his righteousness unto children's children;

Psalm 100:5 – King James Version – [5] For the LORD is good; **his mercy is everlasting;** and his truth endureth to all generations.

Psalm 118:1 – King James Version – O give thanks unto the LORD; for he is good: **because his mercy endureth forever.**

As eternal spirits who are in an eternal relationship with our God who is eternal, all that we do must be considered from the perspective and from the vantage point of our eternity.

Every decision, each choice of conduct and behavior, every thought, action and every desire must be brought into the realm where the standard of eternity becomes our acceptable measure.

The focus statement that "***YOU CANNOT MANAGE WHAT YOU DO NOT MEASURE***" must be our operational guideline, what must base our reality from the perspective and from the vantage point of our eternity.

I am not completely sure why we have not been taught to think and to act eternally. Nor do I know how we have missed the overwhelming volume of information and instructions that are included in the Great Book of Learning about this understanding. The application of eternity to our lives has overwhelming importance for our living and for the outcome of our lives. This knowledge is not new. This has not been added recently; it has always been present in the Book of Kingdoms for our enlightenment and for our benefit. The now, "in-time" references and the world to come "eternal" references are presented many times. The explanation that I have gathered is this:

Our lives on this planet are a brief period "in-time" during our eternity, or during our eternal existence. While we are "in-time" is when we are given the pleasure, the honor and the responsibility of (1) designing, (2) planning (3) and developing what our experience in and for our eternity will be.

Let's consider a few eternal thoughts.

Corinthians 4:18 – King James Version – While we look not at the things which are seen, but at the things which are not seen: for the **things which are seen are temporal;** but the things which **are not seen are eternal.**

1 **Timothy 6:19 – King James Version** – Laying up in store for themselves a good foundation against the time to come, that they may lay hold on eternal life.

Isaiah 9:7 – New Living Translation – His government and its peace will never end. He will rule with fairness and justice from the throne of his ancestor David **for all eternity.** The passionate commitment of the Lord of Heaven's Armies will make this happen.

Isaiah 43:13 – New Living Translation – "From eternity to eternity I am God. No one can snatch anyone out of my hand. No one can undo what I have done."

Daniel 7:14 – New Living Translation – He was given authority, honor and sovereignty over all the nations of the world, so that people of every race and nation and language would obey him. His rule is eternal – it will never end. His kingdom will never be destroyed.

Daniel 4:34 – New Living Translation – I praised and worshiped the Most High and honored the one who lives forever. His rule is everlasting, and his kingdom is eternal.

John 12:25 – New Living Translation – Those who love their life in this world will lose it. Those who care nothing for their life in this world will keep it for eternity.

[2] **Peter 1:11 – New Living Translation** – Then God will give you a grand entrance into the eternal kingdom of our Lord and Savior Jesus Christ.

Revelation 14:6 – New Living Translation – And I saw another angel flying through the sky, carrying the eternal Good News to proclaim to the people who belong to this world – to every nation, tribe, language and people.

IF IT IS NOT ABOUT ETERNITY, IT IS NOT ABOUT KINGDOM.

The dialogue from our Creator and our God is all about eternity. He is everlasting. He is forever. Our relationship with Him is not about temporary things, but the things that are eternal. His love and His mercy endure forever.

We are told to strive with all of our might and all that we have, to be ravenously hungry for His Kingdom, His System, His Plan, His way of doing and being correct. When we go after His Kingdom as our priority and as our primary goal and our sole objective, all of the temporary things (houses, land, clothes, food and anything else that is temporal) will come to us naturally as we seek Him and His way of doing and being right.

Eternity is not our option. We come into life as eternal beings. We live forever. What our experience in our eternity is to be is our choice: whether we choose life or death, blessings or curses, eternal life or eternal damnation. We design our experience "in eternity" while we are "in-time." These are not chosen for us by our Creator/God. The selection of our experience in and for all of our eternity is completely ours.

Since we began our research into eternity as the correct perspective and as the proper vantage point for all of our personal considerations for all of our conduct and for all of our behavior, significant knowledge, wisdom and understanding have been uncovered for all of humanity. I am convinced that this area of our understanding is one of the major efforts and probably the most successful deceits of the defeated Satan. Satan is very good in his strategies and in his deceits to persuade humanity to consider only the temporary that we see with our mortal eyes. The defeated Satan does not want humanity to view our situations, our circumstances and our relationships we experience when we are **"in-time"** from the perspective of eternity. He especially does not want humanity to **view the outcomes** of our conduct and our behavior from the perspective of eternity. The defeated Satan cannot deceive humanity if we choose eternity as our perspective. All of our considerations and our subsequent choices of action must be based in eternity. We must understand and act accordingly, based on the knowledge, the wisdom and from the understanding that life on our planet is only a brief period "in-time" during our eternity, or eternal existence. When we are "in-time" we are given the privilege and the responsibility of designing and developing what our life experience in and for our eternity is to be, **our forever**. This will change everything: our lives will change and our world will change.

Beginning to think **"in eternity"** will not come easy or naturally. A lifetime of incorrect thinking/programming must be changed. It will take effort: concentrated and deliberate effort.

The changes can, will and must happen. The amazing influence and impact on the outcomes of our lives and the lives of those in society whom we are able to influence through our efforts in Kingdom Deployment are worth the effort.

Eternity provides our purpose. Our purpose gives our lives meaning. Our meaning is the source of our hope. We will examine each of these as we progress.

Chapter Three

What Is "*Created Design*"?

Romans 8:28 (based on Amplified)
"We are assured and we know that (a) our God being a partner in their/our labor) that all things work together and are (fitting into a plan) for good to and for good for those who love God and who are called according to (His) created design and for his/their eternal purpose."
(Personal Paraphrase)

Created design can be defined as the unique qualities and the specific characteristics that are given to each of us by our Creator. These talents and gifts are given to us for our engagement and for our deployment into a specific area of service for the Kingdom: government, economy, media, family, education, arts and entertainment, religion and all of the many extensions of these spheres of influence. These qualities provide an anointing of unique favor for enhanced service for the betterment of all of humanity and to bring glory to our God. Operating in our *created design* will present our lives to humanity as a living testament of our God. We will experience a level of personal pleasure and the satisfaction that nothing else can provide. The personal privilege and the unique responsibility of developing these skills to the greatest degree of excellence possible for each of us is for the purpose of our Deployment into our eternal purpose for our Kingdom calling. This understanding is for our deployment into our purpose and for our success in our unique and specific calling. There is a special and unique calling, or a *created design,* for each person for the fulfillment of their purpose in eternity. Nothing under the sun will bring the satisfaction and the experience of contentment to humanity that knowing our *created design* for our eternal purpose and then the living of our life in the pursuit of that endeavor.

> ***Ecclesiastes 3:11 (based on Amplified)***
> ***He has made everything beautiful in its time. He also has planted eternity in men's hearts and minds (as a divinely implanted sense of a purpose working through the ages, generation of time, which nothing under the sun but God alone can satisfy).***
>
> ***(Personal Paraphrase)***

The knowledge that there is a specific *created design* for each of us is not well understood by most of humanity. Many of us begin our lives by observing those around us and deciding what we want to do with our lives, based on our observations of the choices of others and their achieved outcomes. Often, for the first twenty plus years of our lives, we pursue an education solely for our selected employment, based on the achievement of the desired income and the earthly benefits that we want to experience and achieve. This view and this perspective are based completely on horizontal and temporal considerations. These observations act as our motivation for the chosen achievements in our lives. This is decided on by things we see and consider to be what we believe, and what our society perceives as achievements of value. **Sadly, this does not work.** A purely secular or temporal motivation for the success of our lives can provide a chosen lifestyle that often provides excellent benefits, but too often the experience is empty and void of meaning and fulfillment.

Humanity does not do well when our lives do not have meaning, when our lives are just about "things."

Often, the difficulty is that we are not aware that there is a specific and unique *created design* which has been created for us by our Creator/God. We may have a cognitive awareness that something is missing in the experience of the living of our life, but we do not know what we are missing, nor do we know where to look to find what is missing. Sadly, many do not know that they are missing anything. They believe that what they see and experience is all there is to life. They have what we refer to as an incognitive awareness. They do not know that they do not know that there is anything else or that they are missing something important to the enjoyment and success of their lives. They settle for much less than they are designed for.

The Correct Choice to the Alternative Systems of the World

This is not a new or even a recent experience for humanity. When the young rabbi Jesus was traveling near Capernaum more than two thousand years ago, he was teaching about the Kingdom, and healing all who were sick. He had a similar experience. It is stated that when He looked at the crowds who were following Him, He was "moved with compassion because their problems were many and they did not know where to go to get help."

Somehow, in our life experience we have missed the knowledge and the awareness of the beauty and the fulfillment that only a life based on Kingdom Deployment and our *created design* for our eternal purpose delivers to humanity. I do believe that the major disconnect begins with our lack of understanding about eternity. Is it reasonable to believe that the Creator and God, who provides in such detail for our dying and for the ending of our lives on this planet, has not made provision for the beginning and for the successful living of our lives here and now on planet Earth? He is not the God of the sweet by-and-by. He is the God of eternity, "from eternity to eternity," and that very much includes the here and now.

Much needs to be said here to clarify for humanity who our God really is, what He has done and what He has provided for our lives on this planet. This **very** much includes the successful living of our lives **now**.

In one of my favorite chapters in Psalms (139) it is stated that every day of our lives is written in His book before our first day began. He has prepared for us our plan and our purpose. There is meaning for each of our lives. No one is merely here occupying time and space. We have a *created design* for an eternal purpose that goes beyond what we see with our mortal eyes and what we can understand without a correctly programmed mind. How encompassing and how consuming is this relational experience of operating in our *created design* for our eternal purpose? We are told that no matter where we are or where we go, this relationship is there "to guide us and that His strength will support us."

Have you ever been in a really dark place? A place so dark you could not see your hand when you held it up before your face? This is what our God says about that kind of darkness: "I could ask the darkness to hide me and the light around me to become night—but even in darkness I cannot hide from you. To you the night shines as bright as day. Darkness and light are the same to you." There is no darkness that can hide us from Him. He sees us, He guides us and His strength supports us. We cannot hide from Him. Why would we want to hide? His plans for us are for good, for hope, for a future of prosperity and good health and not for disaster. His thoughts about us outnumber the grains of sand. That is a lot. No one can count the grains of sand.

The reality of this relationship and the joy of this experience are challenging for humanity to understand. A spirit that is not in relationship with His Spirit will not understand it. A mind that has not been reprogrammed to think the way that He thinks will not grasp the reality of the vastness of His love for us, nor will they understand His complete provision for all of humanity. The reborn human spirit that has connected (or maybe "reconnected" is a better description) with His Spirit does understand. The human spirit that fellowships directly with Him and with His Spirit operates with joy, with peace, with direction, and with purpose. The darkness from the Kingdom of Darkness cannot hide Him from us. Nor can darkness prevent us from receiving His blessings and His direction for our *created design* for our eternal purpose. This relationship will become easy and natural, Kingdom natural.

We must approach, we must begin and we must operate until the completion of all our relationships are within the relational experience of eternity. We must develop the perspective of eternity and we must operate from the vantage point of eternity. The Holy Spirit God said through Solomon, as recorded in Ecclesiastes, that: "our Creator God has planted eternity and its awareness in our spirit and in our mind to provide us a divinely implanted sense of purpose working in history throughout all time. Nothing under the sun can provide the satisfaction for humanity outside of this experience and this relationship of eternity that is directed by an eternal perspective and from an eternal vantage point."

Created design is the result of understanding our relationship with our Creator. A religious experience will not provide the understanding of our *created design*. Our Creator is not religious. He is relational. If He were religious and concerned only about regulation and compliance with a system of judging and condemning us to punishment, He would have demonstrated that in the Book of Kingdoms. He does not. He does the opposite. Many of those who are listed in the letter to the Hebrews, appropriately named by believers as the Hall of Faith, would not have made the list. The Great Book of Learning, the Book of Kingdoms or the Bible, as many know it, is not a book about religion. It is a book about relationship. Our Creator's love, His desire and His passion for an active, vibrant, living relationship with all of humanity is expressed repeatedly in great detail and with amazing clarity.

The Holy Spirit God, in the letter to the Romans, said something that we often miss.

> ***Romans 8:28 (based on Amplified)***
> ***"We are assured and we know that our (God being a partner in our labor) that all things work together and are (fitting into a plan) for good to and for good for those who love God and who are called according to (His) created design and for His eternal purpose."***
>
> ***(Personal Paraphrase)***

This Scripture says there is an existing plan. This plan exists for us now on planet Earth while we are in the "in-time" experience of our eternity. We do not have to work real hard and struggle to help God create a plan for us; there is and there has been a plan for us from the beginning, from the foundation (eternal) of the earth. God Himself has designed a specific and unique plan for each of us. The plans that He has designed for us are for our good. **(The Plan includes hope and a future of prosperity and good health. We have heard that many times**

before.) We are called according to His design. He created us to complete and to fulfill His plan for us and for our eternal purpose. No one is left out or forgotten in this process. There is design (plan) and purpose (meaning) for each of us.

> **1) The Plan / Knowledge – *The Kingdom System. Facts.***
> **2) His Design / Wisdom – *Kingdomnomics: The Dynamics of Conduct and Behavior.* Personal Application and Engagement**
> **3) His Purpose / Understanding – *Kingdom Deployment: Operating in Your Created Design for Your Eternal Purpose.* Delivering to Society the Kingdom System to Impact Culture.**

What does it mean when He says, "All things?" Does "all things" include everything that we encounter during our lives on this planet? Does this include all of our situations, our circumstances and our relationships while we are "in-time"? Does He say He will make good, be the results for us from everything we experience, from our successes and our failures both good and bad? Is anything that we experience excluded from this declaration of **ALL? NOTHING!**

Why is there such struggle in the pursuit of finding our created design and in the process of determining our eternal purpose? Is it supposed to be that difficult? Is that the design of our Creator? Some even believe it to be impossible. Determining our created design for our eternal purpose is not difficult. Our direction comes from the same letter to the Romans.

Romans 12:2 (Amplified)
"Do not be conformed to this world (this age), [fashioned after and adapted to its external, superficial customs], but be transformed (changed) by the [entire] renewal of your mind [by its new ideals and its new attitude], so that you may prove [for yourselves] **what is the good and acceptable and perfect will of God, even the thing which is good and acceptable and perfect [in His sight for you].**"

Romans 12:2 (New Living Translation)
"Don't copy the behavior and customs of this world, but let God transform you into a new person by changing the way you think. Then you will learn **to know God's will for you, which is good and pleasing and perfect.**"

Ephesians 5:26 (New Living Translation)
"to make her holy and clean, washed by the cleansing of God's word."

Ephesians 5:26 (Amplified)
"So that He might sanctify her, having cleansed her by the washing of water with the Word,"

We must fellowship with our God through His Word. His Word provides clarity and direction for us. We must internalize His Word until it becomes who we are, how we think and what we

believe. His Word provides pinpoint accuracy for our choices in the direction of our life, for the successful outcomes of our life.

Pattern for Relationship:

1) Relationship requires fellowship.

2) Fellowship requires time spent together.

3) Time spent together requires that we give the time.

Chapter Four

Understanding Eternal Purpose

Jeremiah 1:5 (New Living Translation)

"I knew you before I formed you in your mother's womb. Before you were born I set you apart and appointed you as my prophet to the nations."

What is eternal purpose? We have defined eternal or eternity as something that has no beginning and has no ending "in-time." Eternity lasts forever; it always exists and is always true or valid. Purpose is defined as the reason for which someone or something is created. The reason for which someone or something exists. The reason for which something is done in order to achieve or to accomplish an intended or desired result for the end, the aim or the goal of someone or something.

Eternal purpose is the reason for which someone or something exists based on their *created design* in eternity for eternal reasons.

A reason for being is a fundamental and foundational requirement for the success of all of humanity. Our reason for existing provides **purpose** and gives **meaning** to our lives. **Our purpose** provides the **motivation** for our living. When there is **purpose** and when there is **meaning** in our lives we develop **hope**. Our **hope** nurtures and develops our **faith**. Our **faith** is always in something outside of ourselves. This simple yet profound process stimulates our growth as relational beings that are made in the image and in the likeness of our relational Creator God. Our God is totally and completely **relational**.

We have described the process for learning as follows:

(1) Knowledge is knowing the facts.

(2) Wisdom is knowing how the facts apply to you personally.

(3) Understanding is knowing how these facts and how they apply to you personally, fit into our Creator's plan for all of humanity.

Wisdom is completely about you personally, but it never stops only with you. Everything is always about others: how our wisdom impacts those around us and those in need. Our wisdom is for our own benefit and for those who, we share the explanation of how we acquired our knowledge and wisdom, can use our experience to gain direction for understanding their purpose and to give secure meaning to their lives. Our wisdom will assist them in the development of hope for their lives.

The absence of hope in the societies of our world is epidemic. In 2012 on our planet, more than eight hundred thousand of our brothers and sisters ended their own lives. That number is staggering, overwhelming and tragic. The number one reason given by most for ending their lives was because they had no hope. They saw no way out. Life without purpose and without meaning is a life without hope. Life without hope is really not much of a life at all. Humanity requires hope. Hope is the by-product of purpose and meaning. Faith is the by-product of hope.

Humanity so desperately is searching for purpose and for meaning. It appears that many of the traditional sources that we have long believed to be reliable references for determining our life purpose and what we have depended on as trustworthy sources for our personal understanding have failed us. They do not provide accurate input for the success that leads us to the meaning for our lives. They do not lead us to the important understanding that is required for us to determine meaning for our lives. We must have that understanding for the meaning for our lives. Meaning then results in the hope for us that is necessary for success in our lives. What we have included and what we have relied on simply is not working.

Primary among these sources would be religion. Humanity has tried religion and has found that it does not provide the hope it promises. I am not sure this has always been the case.

What has happened? (Research indicates that:)

1) **There are 2.3 billion people on the earth that call themselves followers of Jesus.**
2) **There are five million churches.**
3) **There are forty-three thousand denominations.**
4) **There are twelve million Christian workers.**

Religion is big business. Today religion and its organizations are among the wealthiest and the most powerful organizations on the planet. Religious holdings, religious assets and the related cash flows of religious organizations surpass all other commercial corporations on the planet. The closest organization to religion in holdings and power is government. Government appears to be desperately trying to unseat religion as the wealthiest, most powerful organization on our planet. We have given government a distinct advantage. They can legislate and levy their revenues and they can take property when they decide it is in "their" best interest to do so, "for the greater good."

Sadly, it seems when organizations reach a certain position and a certain size, their growth and their holdings create such demand that self-preservation and self-sustainment becomes their all-consuming mission and their primary objective. Their ability to serve becomes challenged by the overwhelming demands of maintaining the holdings, paying the staff and marketing to keep all the systems going.

This description may not necessarily be categorical. I am

certain there are those who have not lost their focus on humanity and on their call to ministry. The same research from before indicates that 99.7 percent of the ministry produced and the financial support received by organized religion goes to building and maintaining the existing church and to ministering to those who are already engaged in the organizations. That leaves .3 percent to minister to and to reach those who are outside of the existing church. That is three dollars out of each one thousand dollars taken in. Have we lost our way? Has organized religion become a part of the challenge and **not** part of the solution?

Possibly, we have gotten our view and our understanding of the purpose and the function of religion in our lives incorrect. Religion has never been the solution. Religion, when used to point humanity to the God of relationship, can be effective. When religion becomes the substitute to relationship with our Creator God, it will fail us every time. There is no substitute for a personal, living relationship with the true and the living God. A relationship with our God is our only source of hope. Just knowing about our God through religion can and will be frustrating. Our God and our relationship with Him is our only source for hope.

More than a dozen times in the Great Book of Learning we are shown where, before birth, often even before conception, our God tells of a person's birth and provides information about them including their name, their gender and their eternal purpose for being born. I know that was then and this is now. But has our God changed? Does He show partiality? Is that just for "special" people? When He says, "every day of our lives is written in His book before the first day begins," what does He mean? I know we are not robots predestined to act without choice or option. We have choice and free will. I also know that He has told us His plans for us are for good, for hope, for a future of prosperity and good health and He even declares that His plans do not include disaster. What a choice! Life or death / success or failure. **Choose life!**

Humanity often believes that our God is far away and cannot be reached by mortals unless they are something "special." All of the people referenced below are ordinary humans who—it has been proven historically—lived and occupied time on earth. They are like you and me. You are not a surprise to our God, **no matter how you arrived here.** Where you are is not a surprise. Every day of your life is in His book. Every day. Not an occasional day, EVERY day.

Jeremiah 1:5 Young's Literal Translation – "Before I form thee in the belly, I have known thee, and before thou comest forth from the womb I have separated thee, a prophet to nations I have made thee."

Jeremiah 1:15 New Living Translation – "I knew you before I formed you in your mother's womb. Before you were born I set you apart and appointed you as my prophet to the nations."

Galatians 1:15 New Living Translation – "But even before I was born, God chose me and called me by his marvelous grace."

Psalms 139:15, 16 New Living Translation – "You watched me as I was being formed in utter seclusion, as I was woven together in the dark of the womb, You saw me before I was born, Every day of my life was recorded in your book, Every moment was laid out before a single day had passed."

Review these references

Genesis 16:11 – Ishmael
The angel of the LORD said to her further, "Behold, you are with child, And you will bear a son; And you shall call his name Ishmael, Because the LORD has given heed to your affliction.

Genesis 18:10 – Isaac — (Genesis 21:3)
He said, "I will surely return to you at this time next year; and behold, Sarah your wife will have a son." And Sarah was listening at the tent door, which was behind him.

Judges 13:3 – Samson — (Judges 13:24)
Then the angel of the LORD appeared to the woman and said to her, "Behold now, you are barren and have borne no children, but you shall conceive and give birth to a son.

1 Kings 13:2 – Josiah
He cried against the altar by the word of the LORD, and said, "O altar, altar, thus says the LORD, 'Behold, a son shall be born to the house of David, Josiah by name; and on you he shall sacrifice the priests of the high places who burn incense on you, and human bones shall be burned on you.'"

2 Kings 4:16 – Elisha (2 Kings 4:17)
Then he said, "At this season next year you will embrace a son." And she said, "No, my lord, O man of God, do not lie to your maidservant."

Isaiah 9:6 – Jesus
For a child will be born to us, a son will be given to us; And the government will rest on His shoulders; and His name will be called Wonderful Counselor, Mighty God, Eternal Father, Prince of Peace.

Matthew 1:21 – Jesus
"She will bear a Son; and you shall call His name Jesus, for He will save His people from their sins."

Luke 1:13 – John the Baptist
But the angel said to him, "Do not be afraid, Zacharias, for your petition has been heard, and your wife Elizabeth will bear you a son, and you will give him the name John"

1 Samuel 1:11 – Samuel
She made a vow and said, "O LORD of hosts, if You will indeed look on the affliction of Your maidservant and remember me, and not forget Your maidservant, but will give Your maidservant a son, then I will give him to the LORD all the days of his life, and a razor shall never come on his head."

Isaiah 45:1–4 – Cyrus
Thus says the LORD to Cyrus His anointed, whom I have

taken by the right hand, to subdue nations before him And to loose the loins of kings; to open doors before him so that gates will not be shut:"I will go before you and make the rough places smooth; I will shatter the doors of bronze and cut through their iron bars. I will give you the treasures of darkness And hidden wealth of secret places, so that you may know that it is I, the LORD, the God of Israel, who calls you by your name."

He has commanded me to build Him a house at Jerusalem: ***Over one hundred years before Cyrus issued this decree, Isaiah prophesied that the king would make such an order (see Isaiah 44:28; 45:1). Nelson's New King James Version Study Bible.***

Genesis 3: 15 – Jesus

"And I will put enmity between you and the woman, and between your seed and her seed; He shall bruise you on the head, And you shall bruise him on the heel."

Micah 5:1–3 – Jesus

"Now muster yourselves in troops, daughter of troops; They have laid siege against us; With a rod they will smite the judge of Israel on the cheek. But as for you, Bethlehem Ephrathah, too little to be among the clans of Judah, from you One will go forth for Me to be ruler in Israel. His goings forth are from long ago, From the days of eternity." Therefore He will give them up until the time when she who is in labor has borne a child. Then the remainder of His brethren will return to the sons of Israel."

From the beginning, before time, our Creator and our God had your eternal purpose established. He is not striving to see what He can do with you. He is not hoping you will become something. He has your plan. The plan and the purpose of your life is ready to go. The purpose is waiting on you. It is not difficult to discover. He wants you to know.

> ***If you have accepted His grace and you are in right relationship with Him, then follow these simple fellowship steps:***
>
> **1) Relationship requires fellowship.**
>
> **2) Fellowship requires time spent together.**
>
> **3) Time together requires that you give the time.**

There are no shortcuts and no substitutes.

We are told to not copy the behavior and the customs of the world. We must not think like the world thinks. The systems of the world think like the Kingdom of Darkness thinks. We must allow our God to change the way we think, to be like He thinks. Then we will learn to know God's will for us, which is **good** and **pleasing** and **perfect.**

This process causes our thoughts to become agreeable with His will, and our plans are established and our plans succeed.

Knowing and understanding our eternal purpose—the reason for our being—is a fundamental and foundational requirement for our success and for the success of all of humanity. Our reason for existing provides purpose and gives meaning to our lives and provides the motivation necessary for our living. When there is purpose and meaning in our lives we develop hope. Our hope nurtures and develops our faith. Our faith connects to something outside of us. This simple yet profound process stimulates our growth as relational beings who are made in the image and the likeness of our Creator God. Our God is totally and completely relational.

It is completely unreasonable to believe that our Creator/God's plan for us is only to teach us how to die. He came to provide abundant and fulfilling lives now. He is clear. We can and we must believe and we must receive His personal and unique plan for us.

Chapter Five

The Investment Dynamic

How does this relate to Kingdom Deployment?

> ***Revelation 2:26 (Amplified Bible)***
> ***"And he who overcomes (is victorious) and who obeys My commands to the (very) end (doing the works that please Me), I will give him authority and power over the nations."***

Investment can be defined ***as the time, the energy or the matter that we spend in the hope of future benefits.***

The greater the investment that is made, it is understood and expected that the return will be greater. The return on a ten-thousand-dollar investment will yield a greater or larger amount of return than will a ten-dollar investment. Proportionately the yield may be similar, but the amount of the return will be larger because of the larger investment.

Proportionate means keeping the same relationship of size or amount or portion to something else. The amount of yield may have comparable percentages of increase or decrease, but the amount of the yield will be directly related to the amount of the investment.

A dynamic is an interactive system involving competing or conflicting forces. Dynamics operate by design. Our selection, the choice of our actions, is humanity's input, and our decision denotes our choice for a specific, selected outcome.

In our study outlining the vantage point of eternity as our consideration for reviewing our created design for our eternal purpose, the dynamic of investment makes a significant contribution to our understanding of our actual life experiences. Many times in our lives we are faced with challenges. Often the challenges are so unexpected that we are surprised by their occurrences. They appear out of nowhere. The source of the challenge is also many times unexplainable and/or unreasonable. Challenges may come from those with whom we have developed relationships that are important to us: family, friends, church, government, business partners and others. The relationship may become adversarial, and we do not know nor do we understand why. A large number of challenges may be occurring simultaneously; we may be challenged on many different fronts at the same time. It can appear to be unmanageable and overwhelming.

Somehow, many have believed incorrectly that we are not supposed to have challenges. Many believe that the presence of challenge is evidence of something wrong. Often, many believe that the person experiencing the challenge has done something wrong. We may also believe that we should be working towards the time when we will have no challenges.

In the Great Book of Learning or the Book of Kingdoms, from cover to cover we are presented with the reality of our world as a place of continual challenges. It would be difficult to find a single page of the Book where the presence of significant challenges and how to overcome them are not presented. This is not a book about religion and the presentation of do's and don'ts. The Book is not about regulations and our compliance, nor is it about the appointment of earthly judges to oversee humanity's behavior and to keep everyone compliant.

This is the book about two Kingdoms: one King and one who wants to be king, and the epic battle for humanity—challenge after challenge after challenge.

All of the challenges that we will ever encounter in our pursuit of a right relationship with our Creator, who is the true and living King, are addressed. We are shown how to choose the correct conduct and the appropriate behavior in order to accomplish the outcomes we desire for our King and for ourselves.

What does the Dynamic of Investment say about the volume, the frequency, and the magnitude of our challenges from the perspective of the Kingdom of Darkness?

We know what our enemy, the defeated Satan, says about our challenges, and especially the volume, the frequency and the magnitude of our challenges. His strategy and his deceits are to convince those of humanity who are in a relationship with our Creator, the true King, that something is wrong. Something has to be wrong with us. It is not natural for us to have as many challenges as we have, especially challenges of the volume, the magnitude and the frequency that we experience. We have to be doing something wrong. **Most of the time, the opposite is true/correct.**

The defeated Satan works against us by creating situations, circumstances and relationships that he can falsely and incorrectly present to us as a false witness against us. His plans are to make it appear not as it actually is, but instead how he really wants it to be. He creates the confusion in an attempt to present the illusion and the subsequent delusion. All of this is so that he can trick us into believing his lies. There is nothing new here. This was the method he used in the garden.

The Defeated Satan's Pattern – Method of Operation

1) The confusion – Did He say that? What did He really say?
2) The illusion – Why did He say that? He does not want you to be like Him.
3) The delusion – If you listen to me and do what I say, you will be like Him.

All of these efforts are lies for the purpose of creating distortions of reality and to hide the truth. The purpose of his lies is always to deceive and to trick humanity. As with all of his lies, just the opposite of anything that he says is actually true.

What does the Dynamic of Investment say about the volume, the frequency, and the magnitude of our challenges from our perspective of faith?

What we find in the Great Book of Learning is that the volume, the frequency and the magnitude of our challenges are related in direct proportion to the reward that awaits us after we conquer the challenge. Our challenges are the indicators of what our yield will be when we complete the challenges successfully.

In the Parable of the Talents, the servants with five and with two talents doubled their talents. They achieved a 100 percent increase. They were addressed as "good and faithful" and invited to celebrate with the Master. While both the servant with five talents and the servant with two talents garnered the same percentage of increase, the reward of the talent from the unfaithful servant went to the servant with ten talents. This is how redistribution of wealth works in the Kingdom. Observe what the Master said:

28 "Then he ordered, 'Take the money from this servant, and give it to the one with the ten bags of silver.
29 To those who use well what they are given, even more will be given, and they will have abundance. But from those who do nothing, even what little they have will be taken away.' "

Matthew 25:28–29 (New Living Translation)

Earning money is definitely a challenge. Doubling your money is an excellent achievement and a successful result. Both servants were congratulated and honored. It appears that equal honor was given to them based on their increase. The one who had managed the greater amount of challenge was also given an additional talent, or challenge when that was available. He had proven his ability to manage more.

Some may not see talent and/or challenges as rewards or as benefits. The two seem to go together; they appear to be best described as opportunity. Someone said, "If it were easy, everyone would be doing it." Our talents lead us to our challenges. This is always true, without fail. Our challenges lead to our opportunity. Someone else said that our opportunities are wrapped up in hard work.

The young rabbi Jesus states, "To whom much is given, much is required." Great talents require and demand great results.

Luke 12:48 (Amplified Bible)

*"But he who did not know and did things worthy of a beating shall be beaten with few [lashes]. For everyone to whom much is given, of him shall much be required; and of him to whom men entrust much, they will require **and** demand all the more."*

Luke 12:48 (New Living Translation)

"But someone who does not know, and then does something wrong, will be punished only lightly. When someone has been given much, much will be required in return; and when someone has been entrusted with much, even more will be required."

Both talents and challenges are acts of honor for each of us from our Creator. In the Talents Parable it is said that we each receive talents "according to our ability." If you have received the talent, then you have the ability for the talent, or you have the capability of developing the necessary skill for the talent. The ability to hone or to develop our talents is also included in our gifting. We can become better than we are when we begin through our efforts to enhance and to expand our abilities in the areas of our talents.

It has been stated many times that our Creator will not allow more to occur in our lives than we can handle. While this is not in Scripture except in the area of temptation, we are provided a support system to deal with anything that comes to us or at us, no matter the source. The fellowship of believers and the followers of Jesus of Nazareth are described as a living organism, as a body whose primary function is to supply to each part whatever is needed for its successful operation. No one can provide for the need as well as you can. A foot cannot function as a heart.

Psalms 139 says that we can never get away for our Creator, nor will we ever be away from His presence. The experience is graphically described as "If I go up to Heaven, you are there. If I go to the grave, you are there. If I dwell by the farthest ocean, you are there. Wherever I am, there your hand will guide me and your strength will support me."

What we do with our talents and with our challenges represents our investments in the Kingdom Government System of our God. To invest can be defined as ***the time, the energy, or the matter that we spend in the hope of future benefits.***

In our family we have come to understand and to believe that our challenges and their magnitude are directly related to our opportunities and to their rewards for us and for others. While this knowledge and this awareness may not lessen the pain and the disappointment of the present situation, circumstance or relationship, it does give us the ability to see past all of the present reality to an eternal outcome, and can provide much needed hope. The present reality may appear to be pressing. However, we cannot allow the urgency of the present, the "in-time" motivation, to override our primary consideration of eternity as our first determination for all of our actions and our behaviors. The eternal consideration is always more important than the temporal, the "in-time" motivation.

A decision for evil is always based "in-time." Rape, murder, lying, stealing, cheating, homosexuality, abortion, extramarital relations, deception, gossip, abuse and every other evil that you can name are always decided on the basis of an "in-time" motivation.

We are eternal beings. We are in a relationship with an eternal God through His eternal system of government that we know as His Kingdom. We have His eternal Word that describes in great detail how we are to live our lives based in and on our eternity. All of the investments in our lives must be based on our eternity and on our reasoning that is based in eternity. Very little of what we do should ever be based on an "in-time" decision.

Our lives on this planet are a brief period "in-time" during our eternity or during our eternal existence. When we are "in-time" is when we are provided the privilege and the responsibility to plan, to design, and to develop our experience in and for our eternity.

I am not sure how we have missed this. It appears so plain, so fundamental. Yet, little of what humanity does is based on eternity as the motivation.

Chapter Six

Is Eternity Our Option and/or Our Choice?

> ***Matthew 25:46 (New Living Translation)***
> ***"And they will go away into eternal punishment, but the righteous will go into eternal life."***

Definitions

Eternal Spirit – The Spirit of God and the spirit of man are eternal spirits. They are forever. They have no beginning and they have no ending. They exist forever in eternity.

Eternal Life – The provision from the Spirit of the living God for all of humanity enables humanity to fellowship and to communicate directly with our Creator/God. Through this relationship humanity finds their purpose and the meaning for their life "in-time." This understanding provides direction and hope for all of eternity which includes humanity's "in-time" experience.

Eternal Damnation – This is the result of the choice by humanity to not accept the gift of eternal life that is provided for them from our Creator/God. The acceptance of the gift of eternallife results in a living relationship with the true and the living God. The rejection of the gift of eternal life results in the separation forever of humanity from a relationship with our God and from His blessings.

Our spirit is eternal. When our spirit (pneuma', breath) leaves our body (soma, tabernacle), our spirit will return to our Creator/God from whom it came and from where it came. Our body will return to the earth, ash to ash and dust to dust. How do we define this so we will understand the difference between the life that occupies our body when we are born into our "in-time" experience, and the life that then departs our body when we exit or leave this planet? When our "in-time" experience ends, how do we distinguish between the eternal life we have chosen to accept and to develop through a living relationship with our Creator/God? While we are in our "in-time" experience, and the life that comes into and occupies our body while we are born "in-time"? Our reborn spirit that is an eternal relationship with our Creator God will never end. The rebirth of that life/spirit which is already eternal is achieved through our choice to fellowship with the Spirit of the living God. Through this fellowship with the eternal and the living God, our spirit is reborn and humanity is enabled to receive and to experience the gift of eternal life from our Creator/God. Our eternal spirit receives eternal life.

While we are "in-time," our choice is not that of eternity. We are already eternal beings. Our choice is solely what our experience in eternity will be. Will it be eternal life, or will it be eternal damnation? There are only two choices. We have to make a choice. Not making a choice is actually making a choice. A relationship is a choice that requires action.

It is amazing how many times in the Great Book of Learning or the Book of Kingdoms (as I prefer), the distinction and the clarity of our choice is presented.

Let's review a few :

Matthew 25:46 (King James Version) *"And these shall go away into everlasting punishment: but the righteous into life eternal."*

Mark 3:29 (King James Version) *"But he that shall blastpheme against the Holy Ghost hath never forgiveness, but is in danger of eternal damnation."*

John 10:28 (King James Version) *"And I give unto them eternal life; and they shall never perish, neither shall any man pluck them out of my hand."*

John 12:25 (King James Version) *"He that loveth his life shall lose it; and he that hateth his life in this world shall keep it unto life eternal."*

Romans 2:7 (King James Version) *"To them who by patient continuance in well doing seek for glory and honour and immortality, eternal life:"*

Romans 6:23 (King James Version) *"For the wages of sin is death; but the gift of God is eternal life through Jesus Christ our Lord."*

1 Timothy 6:12 (King James Version) *"Fight the good fight of faith, lay hold on eternal life, whereunto thou art also called, and hast professed a good profession before many witnesses."*

1 Timothy 6:19 (King James Version) *"Laying up in store for themselves a good foundation against the time to come, that they may lay hold on eternal life."*

Titus 1:2 (King James Version) *"In hope of eternal life, which God, that cannot lie, promised before the world began;"*

Hebrews 5:9 (King James Version) *"And being made perfect, he became the author of eternal salvation unto all them that obey him;"*

Hebrews 6:2 (King James Version) *"Of the doctrine of baptisms, and of laying on of hands, and of resurrection of the dead, and of eternal judgment."*

Hebrews 9:12 (King James Version) *"Neither by the blood of goats and calves, but by his own blood he entered in once into the holy place, having obtained eternal redemption for us."*

Hebrews 9:15 (King James Version) *"And for this cause he is the mediator of the new testament, that by means of death, for the redemption of the transgressions that were under the first testament, they which are called might receive the promise of eternal inheritance."*

1 John 5:11 (King James Version) *"And this is the record, that God hath given to us eternal life, and this life is in his Son."*

1 John 5:13 (King James Version) *"These things have I written unto you that believe on the name of the Son of God; that ye may know that ye have eternal life, and that ye may believe on the name of the Son of God."*

1 John 5:20 (King James Version) *"And we know that the Son of God is come, and hath given us an understanding, that we may know him that is true, and we are in him that is true, even in his Son Jesus Christ. This is the true God, and eternal life."*

Jude 1:7 (King James Version) *"Even as Sodom and Gomorrha, and the cities about them in like manner, giving themselves over to fornication, and going after strange flesh, are set forth for an example, suffering the vengeance of eternal fire."*

Jude 1:21 (King James Version) "Keep yourselves in the love of God, looking for the mercy of our Lord Jesus Christ unto eternal life."

Matthew 18:8 (New Living Translation) *"So if your hand or foot causes you to sin, cut it off and throw it away. It's better to enter eternal life with only one hand or one foot than to be thrown into eternal fire with both of your hands and feet."*

Matthew 18:9 (New Living Translation) *"And if your eye causes you to sin, gouge it out and throw it away. It's better to enter eternal life with only one eye than to have two eyes and be thrown into the fire of hell."*

Matthew 19:17 (New Living Translation) *"Why ask me about what is good?" Jesus replied. "There is only One who is good. But to answer your question—if you want to receive eternal life, keep the commandments."*

Matthew 25:41 (New Living Translation) *"Then the King will turn to those on the left and say, 'Away with you, you cursed ones, into the eternal fire prepared for the devil and his demons.'"*

Matthew 25:46 (New Living Translation) *"And they will go away into eternal punishment, but the righteous will go into eternal life."*

Mark 9:43 (New Living Translation) *"If your hand causes you to sin, cut it off. It's better to enter eternal life with only one hand than to go into the unquenchable fires of hell with two hands."*

Mark 3:29 (New Living Translation) *"but anyone who blasphemes the Holy Spirit will never be forgiven. This is a sin with eternal consequences."*

Mark 9:45 (New Living Translation) *"If your foot causes you to sin, cut it off. It's better to enter eternal life with only one foot than to be thrown into hell with two feet."*

Mark 10:30 (New Living Translation) *"will receive now in return a hundred times as many houses, brothers, sisters, mothers, children, and property—along with persecution. And in the world to come that person will have eternal life."*

Luke 18:30 (New Living Translation) *"will be repaid many times over in this life, and will have eternal life in the world to come."*

John 3:15 (New Living Translation) *"so that everyone who believes in him will have eternal life."*

John 3:36 (New Living Translation) *"And anyone who believes in God's Son has eternal life. Anyone who doesn't obey the Son will never experience eternal life but remains under God's angry judgment."*

John 5:29 (New Living Translation) *"and they will rise again. Those who have done good will rise to experience eternal life, and those who have continued in evil will rise to experience judgment."*

John 6:63 (New Living Translation) *"The Spirit alone*

gives eternal life. Human effort accomplishes nothing. And the very words I have spoken to you are spirit and life."

Acts 20:26 (New Living Translation) *"I declare today that I have been faithful. If anyone suffers eternal death, it's not my fault"*

Romans 6:21 (New Living Translation) *"And what was the result? You are now ashamed of the things you used to do, things that end in eternal doom."*

Romans 6:22 (New Living Translation) *"But now you are free from the power of sin and have become slaves of God. Now you do those things that lead to holiness and result in eternal life."*

2 Thessalonians 1:9 (New Living Translation) *"They will be punished with eternal destruction, forever separated from the Lord and from his glorious power."*

Titus 3:7 (New Living Translation) *"Because of his grace he declared us righteous and gave us confidence that we will inherit eternal life."*

Hebrews 6:2 (New Living Translation) *"You don't need further instruction about baptisms, the laying on of hands, the resurrection of the dead, and eternal judgment."*

Hebrews 9:15 (New Living Translation) *"That is why he is the one who mediates a new covenant between God and people, so that all who are called can receive the eternal* *inheritance God has promised them. For Christ died to set them free from the penalty of the sins they had committed under that first covenant."*

Jude 1:7 (New Living Translation) *"And don't forget Sodom and Gomorrah and their neighboring towns, which were filled with immorality and every kind of sexual perversion. Those cities were destroyed by fire and serve as a warning of the eternal fire of God's judgment."*

Revelation 17:8 (New Living Translation) *"The beast you saw was once alive but isn't now. And yet he will soon come up out of the bottomless pit and go to eternal destruction. And the people who belong to this world, whose names were not written in the Book of Life before the world was made, will be amazed at the reappearance of this beast who had died."*

The choice is clear. As eternal beings we chose eternal life or eternal damnation.

We have described a learning method that is a practical and experiential process. This is a method where you can experience outcomes practically, in benefit and in relationship. The steps are:

1) Knowledge – knowing the facts.
2) Wisdom – knowing how the facts apply to you personally.
3) Understanding – knowing how the facts and how they apply to you personally, fit into our Creator's plan and purpose for all of humanity.

Every choice that we make must be based on eternity and on the eternal consequences of our thoughts, our actions and our desires. Yet it appears that little or, maybe more accurately, none of our conduct nor any of our behavior is considered from the perspective of eternity and from it's eternal consequences. We must consider the eternal outcomes of our actions that we have chosen before we act. The consequences of ignoring eternity and deciding our course of action based solely on our "in-time" motivation can be seen all around us and in every area of our lives.

When we examine our life experiences, it is not difficult to recognize whether our choices have been made from the vantage point of eternity, or if our motivation is from an "in-time" perspective. The consideration of eternity will produce eternal results that will lead to an outcome which is good for us and good for humanity. "In-time" actions that are based on selfish desires are centered and based on immediate self-satisfaction and self-gratification. They are usually achieved at someone else's expense.

We have not been instructed nor have we been taught the ways of eternity. Because we are not readily familiar with our actions from our eternal perspective and because we do not understand the terms of eternity and because we cannot readily compare our choices to our "in-time" motivations, we often miss the eternal influence and we overlook the difference and the impact on our lives. Most of our actions are decided solely from an "in-time" motivation. "In-time" is the way of the world; this is how the world operates. This is how the Kingdom of Darkness operates; this is not the way of the Kingdom of Light.

There are major differences in the results and in the outcomes of the decisions we choose that are based on our "in-time" thoughts and considerations, and those we choose when we base our considerations and actions on eternity. The outcomes are easy to see and not difficult to distinguish between the sources of our motivation. You do not have to be a scholar nor do you have to be a genius. You simply have to be informed of the two choices and then be aware that in every decision we make, we choose our decision based on one or the other—"in-time" or "in-eternity." This reality affects every thought, every action and every desire of our life on this planet. Let's review a few and determine if our choices are "in-time" or eternally based motivation.

Debt – A debt generally refers to money owed by one party, the debtor, to a second party, the creditor. Debt is generally subject to contractual terms regarding the amount, timing and repayment of principal and interest.

Debt in our world is out of control. The site, www.nationaldebtclocks.org will provide a visual perspective of the debt of the nations in our world. Debt is out of control in the societies of the world. Debt is a noose around the necks of our societies. Debt is a scourge on humanity. Debt is no longer manageable for most nations nor for most individuals. If creditors were to make demand for repayment, we the debtors would not be able to repay.

Why do we have debt? Is our choice for debt motivated by an existing need for the engaging in our created design for the fulfilling of our eternal purpose where we fully consider the impact of debt on our eternal outcomes? Or is debt motivated by a short-term perceived need that we consider important, based on our immediate gratification?

Is debt a matter of choice? Can we choose to not have debt? Can we manage our revenues and our resources to operate and to grow within the capacity of our available assets without incurring debt, and still be successful? What does it mean "to owe no man anything but to love them?" Is the borrower really a "servant to the lender"?

Debt in the Kingdom of Darkness is not meant to be a way to bless you or to provide a method for you to get ahead. Every contract that is written is skewed toward the lender. The contract reserves broad rights for the lender and takes away most of the rights of the borrower. Most of these rights can be exercised unilaterally at the discretion of the lender.

Debt can and should be avoided as much as possible.

Character – Character is defined as the moral and/or the ethical qualities that form the basic or inherent features of an individual or a group.

It is stated often that our world is experiencing a leadership crisis. The saying by Lord Acton that "all power tends to corrupt and absolute power corrupts absolutely" shines the spotlight on the real challenge. John Adams expanded the observation as follows: "Because power corrupts, society's demand for moral authority and character increase as the importance of the position increases."

Without an established standard of truth, humanity tends to seek everything for their personal advantage. Truth is unchanging. It is and has remained the same since before the creation of time. Ravi Zacharias, a Master Teacher, presents a valid consideration:

"If we choose to live our existence without any transcendent point of reference, we have no point of testing what really defines the most critical questions of life."

We become our own god and we formulate and live by our own truth. Ravi Zacharias further expounds on what is happening in the United States presently. These are fundamental and foundational questions that focus and direct our lives correctly, for an honorable and desirable outcome. They are questions that must be asked and that also must be answered correctly.

"As you look upon this country now and what's happened in the last four decades, we are very cognizant of a serious war raging thousands of miles away that threatens our lifestyle and the values we cherish. But there is a more insidious war going on right in the home front. To what source are we going to look for objective moral authority and value? What is going to define us as a people?"

What is our character choice when we consider eternity? Are the choices of character for eternity debatable? Does the consideration of eternity make our choices more clearly defined?

Fidelity – Fidelity is defined as faithfulness to a person, a cause or a belief that is demonstrated by continuing loyalty and support.

> *"Many persons have a wrong idea of what constitutes true happiness. It is not attained through self-gratification but through fidelity to a worthy purpose."*
> Helen Keller

"Faithful women are all alike, they think only of their fidelity, never of their husbands."
Jean Giraudoux

"Not observation of a duty but liberty itself is the pledge that assures fidelity."
Ellen Key

"Fidelity is the sister of justice."
Horace

"In the last analysis, of course, an oath will encourage fidelity in office only to the degree that officeholders continue to believe that they cannot escape ultimate accountability for a breach of faith."
James L. Buckley

Fidelity is an eternal decision.

Integrity – Integrity is defined as the quality of being honest and having strong moral principles; moral uprightness.

"Goodness is about character – integrity, honesty, kindness, generosity, moral courage and the like. More than anything else, it is about how we treat other people."
Dennis Prager

"The greatness of a man is not in how much wealth he acquires, but in his integrity and his ability to affect those around him positively."
Bob Marley

"Live so that when your children think of fairness, caring, and integrity, they think of you."
H. Jackson Brown

"The supreme quality for leadership is unquestionably integrity. Without it, no real success is possible, no matter whether it is on a section gang, a football field, in an army, or in an office."
Dwight D. Eisenhower

"Real integrity is doing the right thing, knowing that nobody's going to know whether you did it or not."
Oprah Winfrey

"With integrity, you have nothing to fear, since you have nothing to hide. With integrity, you will do the right thing, so you will have no guilt."
Zig Ziglar

"The time you spend alone with God will transform your character and increase your devotion. Then your integrity and godly behavior in an unbelieving world will make others long to know the Lord."
Charles Stanley

"If you don't have integrity, you have nothing. You can't buy it. You can have all the money in the world, but if you are not a moral and ethical person, you really have nothing."
Henry Kravis

Each decision about integrity is an eternal decision.

Morality – Morality is defined as principles concerning the distinction between right and wrong or good and bad behavior; a particular system of values and principles of conduct and behavior.

> *"A man does what he must—in spite of personal consequences, in spite of obstacles and dangers and pressures—and that is the basis of all human morality."*
> Winston Churchill

> *"When you think of it, really there are four fundamental questions of life. You've asked them, I've asked them, every thinking person asks them. They boil down to this: origin, meaning, morality and destiny. 'How did I come into being? What brings life meaning? How do I know right from wrong? Where am I headed after I die?'"*
> Ravi Zacharias

> *"Morality which depends upon the helplessness of a man or woman has not much to recommend it. Morality is rooted in the purity of our hearts."*
> Mahatma Gandhi

> *"Let us with caution indulge the supposition that morality can be maintained without religion. Reason and experience both forbid us to expect that national morality can prevail in exclusion of religious principle."*
> George Washington

"The greatest tragedy in mankind's entire history may be the hijacking of morality by religion."
Arthur C. Clarke

"Compassion is the basis of morality."
Arthur Schopenhauer

"Science is the search for truth, that is, the effort to understand the world: it involves the rejection of bias, of dogma, of revelation, but not the rejection of morality."
Linus Pauling

"Morality is the basis of things and truth is the substance of all morality."
Mahatma Gandhi

"Ordinary morality is only for ordinary people."
Aleister Crowley

"Aim above morality. Be not simply good, be good for something."
Henry David Thoreau

Morality is an eternal choice.

Honor – To regard with great respect; to fulfill an obligation or to keep an agreement.

"You will never do anything in this world without courage. It is the greatest quality of the mind next to honor."
Aristotle

"All the great things are simple, and many can be expressed in a single word: freedom, justice, honor, duty, mercy, hope."
Winston Churchill

"Confidence ... thrives on honesty, on honor, on the sacredness of obligations, on faithful protection and on unselfish performance. Without them it cannot live."
Franklin D. Roosevelt

"No person was ever honored for what he received. Honor has been the reward for what he gave."
Calvin Coolidge

"I love the name of honor, more than I fear death."
Julius Caesar

"The greatest way to live with honor in this world is to be what we pretend to be."
Socrates

"When the will defies fear, when duty throws the gauntlet down to fate, when honor scorns to compromise with death – that is heroism."
Robert Green Ingersoll

"Duty, Honor, Country. Those three hallowed words reverently dictate what you ought to be, what you can be, what you will be."
Douglas MacArthur

"The battle of life is, in most cases, fought uphill; and to win it without a struggle were perhaps to win it without honor. If there were no difficulties there would be no success; if there

were nothing to struggle for, there would be nothing to be achieved."
Samuel Smiles

"I take things like honor and loyalty seriously. It's more important to me than any materialistic thing or any fame I could have."
Lloyd Banks

"It is not the honor that you take with you, but the heritage you leave behind."
Branch Rickey

Honor requires an eternal consideration.

Sexuality Choices – Sexuality is a huge business in our world. The Kingdom of Darkness makes all of the sexual choices about personal pleasure, personal satisfaction and personal gratification. The Church world and religion make all of the choices about sin. The battle between the two schools of thought rages, and humanity is most often the victim and the one who suffers and loses. Solomon said that anything sounds correct until one knows the facts.

LET'S CONSIDER THE BIG THREE.

A) Extramarital sex – Today we have an orphan epidemic. The number of orphans in the world is approaching 200 million. Men deposit their seed anywhere and everywhere, with their only consideration being personal pleasure and self-gratification. Their seed has no value to them.

B) Homosexuality – Many of humanity's brightest and most capable potential contributors to society and to posterity select a lifestyle that does not permit them to participate in the betterment and the advancement of all of humanity on our planet through procreation. Understanding created design and eternal purpose shines the light on our individuality and on the specific value of each of humanity as seen for society and posterity. It is not just about us, but it is completely about us. We are contributors; we are participants in the quality of the life experience on our planet for all of humanity. We do this through our seed. Through the nurturing, the development and through our imparting of all that we are to our seed. Then our seed will in turn do the same for their seed. One of humanity's greatest pleasures is to see our seed and our seed's seed becoming successful and contributing to the betterment and to the advancement of the life experiences of our world for all of humanity. Our seed is a special gift to us from our God. Our seed is one of the most valuable things we will ever have.

C) Abortion – No single act better presents the lack of value that our societies and our cultures place on their seed. In America alone more than 60 million lives have been ended with the primary reasoning of inconvenience. When does life begin? We have read that before we are in our mother's womb our Creator knows our name. He has the days of our lives written in His book before the first day begins. There are no accidents. No matter how the seed gets there, it is no surprise to our Creator/God. His plans for all seed are for good, for hope and for a future of prosperity and good health. The temporary situations, circumstances and relationships of the seed do not change nor do they impact the eternal purpose of our Creator God for all seed. Our enemy, the defeated Satan, wants to destroy our seed and to steal our heritage in order to take away our contribution through our seed. We must not allow temporary situations, circumstances and relationships to take away our eternal heritage. Abortion is a temporary decision that has eternal outcomes.

ALL OF THESE ARE ETERNAL DECISIONS.

Dress/Appearance – The late Dr. Myles Munroe put this simply and accurately. He said, "Dress the way you want to be addressed."

Our appearance reflects our views of eternity.

Good Judgments – Drugs, alcohol, food – The ability to make considered decisions or come to sensible conclusions.

There are many situations, circumstances and relationships that we encounter, and each must be viewed from the perspective of eternity. This is a major area where we have the privilege, the honor and the responsibility to reprogram our minds. We must think the way our God thinks, and He thinks in eternity.

It is not difficult to see or to understand why our enemy, the defeated Satan, wants our consideration and our concentration to be "in-time" and not "in eternity." Our "in-time" experience on this planet is only a brief period of time during our eternity, or eternal existence. "In-time" is when we design and develop what our experience in eternity will be.

We are eternal spirits. We are in relationship with an eternal Creator/God. Our eternal spirit accepts the gift of eternal life from our Creator, and we fellowship with Him directly for eternity, Spirit to spirit. He has given us His eternal Word so that we can understand Him and His plan for all of humanity, both individually and collectively. He has given us His Spirit, His eternal Kingdom Government, so that we can engage all the power of Heaven, the Angel Armies of God, and invite the Holy Spirit God to intervene in our situations, our circumstances and in our relationships for our victory.

He has told us that His plans for us are for good, for hope and for a future of prosperity and good health. Disaster is not part of His plan for us. He has declared that in every situation we are made to triumph through Christ Jesus. We tread upon serpents and scorpions and over all of the power of the enemy. He has given us the shield of faith so that we may quench every fiery dart of the defeated Satan. Greater is He who is living in us and working through us than he that is in the world.

No weapon formed against us will prosper. A thousand may fall at our side and ten thousand at our right hand, but it will not come near us. When our enemy comes at us from one direction, He sends them scattering in seven directions. If our enemy persists, He will destroy him before our very eyes.

We recognize the strategies and the deceits of the defeated Satan and we put a stop to them by speaking His Word out of our mouth in faith.

We are renewing our minds and changing the way we think so that we think like our God thinks. We are what He says we are and we have what He says that we have. We can and we will do what He says that we can do.

Through our renewed minds that we are washing continually with the water of the Word of our God, He causes our thoughts to become agreeable with His will, and our plans are established and we succeed.

The Scripture below presents insight for us into our position in Christ:

> **Romans 8:28 (based on Amplified)**
> ***"We are assured and We know that our Creator (God being a partner in our labor) that all things that we experience work together and are (fitting into a plan) for <u>good</u> to and for good <u>for</u> those who love God and who are called according to (His) Created design and for His eternal purpose."***
> ***(Personal Paraphrase)***

Romans 8:28

1) God is partnering with us.
2) God is our partner.
3) All things are working together into a plan for us.
4) The plan is good to us and good for us because we love God.

5) He has called and created us for His specific design for His eternal purposes.

We are the product of created design and we are designed specifically for our eternal purpose. When we operate in our created design, we are partnering with our Creator, God.

Chapter Seven

The Necessity of Purpose

Ecclesiastes 3:11 (based on Amplified)
"He has made everything beautiful in its time. He also has planted eternity in men's hearts (spirits) and in their minds. Eternity provides a divinely implanted sense of purpose that works through the ages (generations of time) which nothing under the sun but God alone can satisfy."
(Personal Paraphrase)

Purpose is the reason for someone or something's being: the cause, the explanation, and the justification for their existence.

Having purpose is enormously important for humanity. Purpose has direct impact on human longevity as well as on their quality of life. Much research supports this understanding.

Purpose is a key ingredient for balance and for success in everyone's life—no matter what their socioeconomic standing, their race, gender, height, skills, position in employment, education or any other defining descriptions used to describe who a person is. A clear purpose is the necessary ingredient for their success.

We have observed this in all social and economic levels of humanity, from the wealthiest to the poorest and everyone in between. Those with tremendous wealth, whether inherited or earned, can easily arrive at a life experience where they believe that nothing has meaning. Everything is empty. Solomon, the king of Israel, who experienced one of the most lavish and extreme pleasure-driven lives that has ever been recorded, came to the place where he believed and stated repeatedly that nothing had meaning: "Vanity of vanities, all is vanity." Those with great wealth can purchase the sensory or sensual pleasures they desire. All of these pleasures soon become empty and without joy. Sadly, many discover that the small amount which satisfied them initially, now requires a much larger quantity to produce the same experience. This is the case with alcohol, drugs, pornography, sexuality, power, lust, fame and many other substitutes that are used to replace their experience of understanding their created design for their eternal purpose. Often their cravings escalate so much that they require a lethal dose to satisfy themselves, and that is what takes their lives. How tragic. The pursuit of anything as a substitute for knowing your created design for your eternal purpose and following that effort will only produce frustration and disappointment, and will lead to the deception of a hopeless feeling or the perception of defeat in one's mind.

Those on the other end of the economic spectrum, who have no money and no wealth, often believe that they cannot compete. The gap is too wide, the mountain too high, and they cannot make it all work for them. It is useless to try. Interestingly, the substitutes for purpose are the same for both economic groups. Alcohol, drugs, pornography, sexuality, power, lust and fame are the leading choices for both groups. Each economic group has their unique manner of dealing with the frustration and the feelings of defeat that no clear purpose brings to our lives. All choices usually reflect extremes on each respective level. How tragic.

There appears to be a pattern here for everyone.

1) **Purpose provides meaning.**
2) **Meaning produces positive motivation.**
3) **Motivation (a reason to act) provides hope.**
4) **Hope nurtures and develops faith.**
5) **Faith leads us to a source and a relationship from a source that is outside of ourselves, someone greater and more capable than we are.**

This book is about deployment, and deployment has its underlying support and foundation on the basis of eternity. All of the substitutes we can possibly imagine and could ever engage, including those listed here, address only our "in-time" experience and are meant to satisfy our perceived "in-time" need. Isn't it interesting that the Holy Spirit God, through Solomon, stated that

"He made everything beautiful in its time." I recall a conversation with my son, when the beauty and the pleasurable emotions and the physical good feelings that the choices of bad conduct and bad behavior deliver to humanity were being discussed. Extramarital sexual relationships often involve two attractive people. The temporary pleasure of the physical experience can be ecstatic and often produces temporary, over whelming happiness and a joyful excitement, almost euphoric. However, when we consider the actual cost for humanity, it is not difficult to see that the price is too great. Such experiences have produced tens of millions of fatherless children who are struggling to survive without the relationship of a loving father. A father to nurture and to guide them, someone to impart wisdom and understanding to them. The number of orphans in our world is quickly approaching 200 hundred million.

All of the advertisements about alcohol show the coolest people in the neatest situations. Everyone would want to experience what they are experiencing. In all of the advertising, alcohol consumption appears so attractive, so desirable. Their marketing is working.

The statistics are staggering. On their website, the National Institutes of Health's presentation on "Alcohol Abuse and Alcoholism in the United States" describes the tragic outcomes of humanity who are deceived by the marketing of the alcohol industry. There are so many.

This information is important for our understanding, so I am including some of the highlights.

Alcohol Use in the United States:

Prevalence of Drinking:

In 2012, 87.6 percent of people ages 18 or older reported that they drank alcohol at some point in their lifetime; 71 percent reported that they drank in the past year; 56.3 percent reported that they drank in the past month.

Prevalence of Binge Drinking and Heavy Drinking:

In 2012, 24.6 percent of people ages 18 or older reported that they engaged in binge drinking in the past month; 7.1 percent reported that they engaged in heavy drinking in the past month.

Alcohol Use Disorders (AUDs) in the United States:

Adults (ages 18+): Approximately 17 million adults ages 18 and older (7.2 percent of this age group) had an AUD in 2012. This includes 11.2 million men (9.9 percent of men in this age group) and 5.7 million women (4.6 percent of women in this age group).

• About 1.4 million adults received treatment for an AUD at a specialized facility in 2012 (8.4 percent of adults in need). This included 416,000 women (7.3 percent of women in need) and 1.0 million men (8.9 percent of men in need).

Youth (ages 12–17): In 2012, an estimated 855,000 adolescents ages 12–17 (3.4 percent of this age group) had an AUD. This number includes 444,000 females (3.6 percent) and 411,000 males (3.2 percent).

- An estimated 76,000 adolescents received treatment for an AUD at a specialized facility in 2012 (8.9 percent of adolescents in need). This included 28,000 females (6.3 percent of adolescent females in need) and 48,000 males (11.7 percent of adolescent males in need).

Alcohol-Related Deaths:

Nearly 88,000 people (approximately 62,000 men and 26,000 women) die from alcohol-related causes annually, making it the third leading preventable cause of death in the United States.

In 2012, alcohol-impaired-driving fatalities accounted for 10,322 deaths (31 percent of overall driving fatalities).

Economic Burden:

In 2006, alcohol misuse problems cost the United States $223.5 billion. Almost three-quarters of the total cost of alcohol misuse is related to binge drinking.

Global Burden:

In 2012, 3.3 million deaths, or 5.9 percent of all global deaths (7.6 percent for men and 4 percent for women), were attributable to alcohol consumption. Alcohol contributes to over 200 diseases and injury-related health conditions, most notably alcohol dependence, liver cirrhosis, cancers, and injuries. In 2012, alcohol accounted for 5.1 percent of disability-adjusted life years (DALYs) worldwide. Globally, alcohol misuse is the fifth leading risk factor for premature death and disability; among people between the ages of 15 and 49, it is the first.

Family Consequences:

More than 10 percent of U.S. children live with a parent with alcohol problems, according to a 2012 study.

Underage Drinking:

Prevalence of Underage Alcohol Use:

- ***Prevalence of Drinking:*** 2 out of 5 15-year-olds report that they have had at least one drink in their lives. In 2012, about 9.3 million people ages 12–20 (24.3 percent of this age group) reported drinking alcohol in the past month (24.7 percent of males and 24 percent of females).
- ***Prevalence of Binge Drinking:*** Approximately 5.9 million people (about 15 percent) ages 12–20 were binge drinkers (16.5 percent of males and 14 percent of females).
- ***Prevalence of Heavy Drinking:*** Approximately 1.7 million people (about 4.3 percent) ages 12–20 were heavy drinkers (5.2 percent of males and 3.4 percent of females).

Consequences of Underage Alcohol Use:

Research indicates that alcohol use during the teenage years could interfere with normal adolescent brain development and increase the risk of developing an AUD. In addition, underage drinking contributes to a range of acute consequences, including injuries, sexual assaults, and even deaths.

Alcohol and College Students:

Prevalence of Alcohol Use:

- ***Prevalence of Drinking:*** In 2012, 60.3 percent of

college students ages 18–22 drank alcohol in the past month compared with 51.9 percent of same-age peers not in college.

• ***Prevalence of Binge Drinking:*** 40.1 percent of college students ages 18–22 engaged in binge drinking (5 or more drinks on an occasion) in the past month compared with 35 percent of same-age peers not in college.

• ***Prevalence of Heavy Drinking:*** 14.4 percent of college students ages 18–22 engaged in heavy drinking (5 or more drinks on an occasion, on 5 or more occasions per month) in the past month, compared with 10.7 percent of same-age peers not in college.

Consequences – Researchers estimate that each year:

• 1,825 college students between the ages of 18 and 24 die from alcohol-related unintentional injuries, including motor vehicle crashes.

• 696,000 students between the ages of 18 and 24 are assaulted by another student who has been drinking.

• 97,000 students between the ages of 18 and 24 report experiencing alcohol-related sexual assault or date rape.

• Roughly 20 percent of college students meet the criteria for an AUD.

• About 1 in 4 college students reports academic consequences from drinking, including missing class, falling behind in class, doing poorly on exams or papers and receiving lower grades overall.

Alcohol and Pregnancy:

The prevalence of fetal alcohol syndrome (FAS) in the United States was estimated by the Institute of Medicine in 1996 to be between 0.5 and 3.0 cases per 1,000.

More recent reports from specific U.S. sites found the prevalence of FAS to be 2 to 7 cases per 1,000, and the prevalence of fetal alcohol spectrum disorders (FASD) to be as high as 20 to 50 cases per 1,000.

Alcohol and the Human Body:

Among all cirrhosis deaths in 2009, 48.2 percent were alcohol related. The proportion of alcohol-related cirrhosis was highest (70.6 percent) among decedents ages 35–44.

In 2009, alcohol-related liver disease was the primary cause of almost 1 in 3 liver transplants in the United States.

Alcohol has been identified as a risk factor for the following types of cancer: mouth, esophagus, pharynx, larynx, liver and breast.

Our adversary, the defeated Satan, is slick. He makes things that will destroy us and our families appear to be so innocent and so harmless, they even appear to be fun. Alcohol is a temporary "in-time" choice with eternal consequences for us, for those that we love and for all of the community of humanity.

> ***Proverbs 20:1 (The Message)***
> ***"Wine makes you mean, beer makes you quarrelsome—a staggering drunk is not much fun."***
>
> ***Proverbs 20:1 (New Living Translation)***
> ***"Wine produces mockers; alcohol leads to brawls Those led astray by drink cannot be wise."***

ALCOHOL IS THE MOST ABUSED DRUG IN OUR SOCIETIES.

There appears to be much debate in the United States about drugs and their usage. Marijuana is the poster child and is held up as a harmless drug with no consequences. Statistics do not support that theory. Marijuana is a proven gateway drug that leads to using other drugs. The negative impact of prolonged and repeated use of marijuana on a user's body and on their mind is tragic. The choice to use drugs is a lawless act. In the Great Book of Learning we are told to honor and to obey the laws of our country. To intentionally disobey laws is an act of rebellion and there are consequences. You will not escape them.

Pornography impacts humanity much like drugs. You start off lightly dabbling in pornography, but soon you have to go deeper, to the most horrible and horrific forms of abuse to be satisfied. I recall Ted Bundy, the mass murderer who had wreaked havoc on college campuses, stating that his involvement with "girlie magazines" led him to engage in more perverse activities, which eventually led to where he committed rape, murder and incest to satisfy his out-of-control lusts. In an interview just before his execution, Bundy asked his interviewer to please tell others about the trap that any involvement in pornography sets for humanity.

Bundy's activities began with masturbation. The unreal and phony imagination that is involved in masturbation makes it difficult for a real experience to compete and to satisfy the individual's lust.

Just a little extramarital sex, just a little alcohol, just a little marijuana, just a little pornography, just a little lie, just a little cheating, just steal a little, just a little abortion, just a little homosexuality ... all of this is part of the master plan of our enemy. The defeated Satan plans all to trick and to deceive us. His purpose is to kill our influence, to steal our potential and to destroy our lives. It is our legacy and our heritage that he wants to take from us.

A fire is a beautiful thing. In the right place, it is beautiful to watch and nice to enjoy its warmth. But even the smallest fire in the wrong place, in the middle of your home, will burn your home to the ground and destroy your personal place of sanctuary.

Do not be fooled. Stay away; have nothing to do with the choices whose engagements have the capacity and the capability to destroy everything. We are not stupid. We are programmed to make good choices.

We must take the time necessary to fellowship with our Creator God. He wants to know us, and He wants us to really know Him, not just to know about Him. There is a plan for us. We are uniquely designed to fulfill this plan. This created design will lead us to fulfill our planned eternal purpose. We will not be easily swayed by temporary situations, circumstances or relationships that entice us to make unwise choices based completely on present pressures. Our experiences "in-time" and for eternity will be directed by our knowledge of the plan that is specifically designed for us. The understanding of our purpose will lead to a satisfying and rewarding life.

Life is about eternity. Our most important consideration for all of our life on this planet is eternity.

Chapter Eight

The Loss and the Absence of Hope

> ***Hebrews 11 (based on The Voice)***
> ***"Faith is the assurance of things you have hoped for (or are hoping for), and the absolute conviction that there are realities that you have never seen."***
> ***(Personal Paraphrase)***

Hope – The feeling that what is wanted or that our events will turn out for the best.

Trust, reliance – Desire that is accompanied by expectation of or belief in the fulfillment.

Absence - A lack of something; when something is missing or not present.

Loss – The fact or process of losing something.

The state or feeling of grief when deprived of something.

"Hope deferred makes the heart sick, but a dream fulfilled is a tree of life." Proverbs 13:12 – New Living Translation

"Unrelenting disappointment leaves you heartsick, but a sudden good break can turn life around. Proverbs 13:12 – The Message"

Solomon said that we should make it our priority to protect our spirit (heart), because out of our spirit flows all of the issues of our life. One translation says to guard your heart above all else, for it determines the course (the route or direction) of all of your life. Other versions say that out of our spirit flows the wellspring (the origin and the bountiful source) of life and that out of it are the outgoings (a person's regular expenditure) of life.

What we will examine now is where hope comes from and how hope is cultivated and maintained. We will determine the evidence of lost hope and the resulting outcomes when hope is absent. We will close our study with the understanding of how to regain our hope.

In the previous chapter we discussed a pattern that we believe most of humanity follows in their experience of living life with purpose.

1) **Purpose provides meaning.**
2) **Meaning produces positive motivation.**
3) **Motivation (a reason to act) produces hope.**
4) **Hope nurtures and develops faith.**
5) **Faith leads us to a source and a relationship outside of ourselves, someone greater and more capable than ourselves.**

A component is a part or an element of a larger whole. If any of the components in this process are missing, the entire system falls apart. It will not work. When we understand what knowledge is to our good health—spirit, mind and body—we become aware of the necessity of having accurate facts, facts, for each of us to gain the correct wisdom for our living. We then understand and we then know that we cannot bypass or leave out any of these steps. When any of the components are missing, there are unhealthy consequences in our life experiences.

Having purpose provides meaning for our existence. The meaning that we receive from purpose provides the motivation for us to act or, more simply, to be engaged and to do something. Our action is reflective of the presence of hope and is evidence that we believe that the results we desire are achievable and we believe results will follow. Faith is a major component of hope. Faith is always personal and begins completely with the individual. Faith does not end with the individual. It will always begin there, but faith will always lead you outside of yourself to a relationship with a higher authority and a greater power that has influence in the outcomes of your purposes.

Where does hope come from? Below are some of the thoughts from the Scriptures in the Great Book of Learning.

- "My hope is in you all day long." *Psalm 25:5*
- "May integrity and uprightness protect me, because my hope is in you." *Psalm 25:21*

- "Be strong and take heart, all you who hope in the LORD." *Psalm 31:24*
- "We wait in hope for the LORD; he is our help and our shield." *Psalm 33:20*
- "May your unfailing love rest upon us, O LORD, even as we put our hope in you." *Psalm 33:22*
- "I will praise you forever for what you have done; in your name I will hope, for your name is good." "I will praise you in the presence of your saints." *Psalm 52:9*
- "Find rest, O my soul, in God alone; my hope comes from him." *Psalm 62:5*
- "But as for me, I will always have hope; I will praise you more and more." *Psalm 71:14*
- "You are my refuge and my shield; I have put my hope in your word." *Psalm 119:114*
- "I wait for the LORD, my soul waits, and in his word I put my hope." *Psalm 130:5*

Life on our planet is primarily a practical experience that involves contact with others. It is our observation that contact is about relationship. Relationship is important. Relationships do not work without faith. Where there is no faith, there is no relationship. To enter into an agreement or a partnership where there is no faith and no hope can be an unhealthy and unwise decision. You may go through the motions, but without faith this is an empty experience. You cannot be in a relationship without faith. It is impossible to experience faith without hope being present. In the most fundamental of transactions, faith and hope are integral components. In the voice translation of Hebrews, the correlation and the connection between faith and hope are expressed well.

> ***Hebrews 11:1 (based on The Voice)***
> ***"Faith is the confident assurance of things that you have hoped for (or are hoping for), and the absolute conviction that there (they) are realities that you have never seen."***
> ***Personal Paraphrase***

Hope that is lasting and hope that is real is produced only from our spirit. Our mind is the gateway through which faith and hope enter. Real hope, or hope that is genuine, is the product of our renewed mind. When our mind has been correctly reprogrammed through our correctly inputting accurate and factual information, our thoughts and our considerations agree with what our Creator says and what He has said. Is this important? Dr. Myles Munroe has said that "our challenge in life is not who we are, but who we believe that we are."

Hope is cultivated by fellowshipping with our Creator, with His Word and with His Spirit. We must spend time with Him, time with His Word and time with His Spirit. Our faith comes to us when we hear His Word. He is the author and the developer of our faith. We must provide/furnish/give the time that is necessary in order to allow our spirit and our mind to get to know our Creator.

Attending meetings or gatherings where we simply learn about Him is not enough. There is a vast difference between knowing about someone and knowing them personally. The relationship process that we have identified is as follows:

> **1) Relationship requires fellowship.**
>
> **2) Fellowship requires that we spend time together.**
>
> **3) Spending time together requires that we give the time.**

Why is it so difficult for us to give the time? I believe we allow the temporary things, the "in-time" things of our lives, the things that are sensory—touch, taste, seeing, feeling and hearing—to consume our thoughts and to dominate and to control our actions. We become too busy with temporary things and we do not direct ourselves to consider eternity first and primarily.

There is absolutely nothing more important and nothing that is more necessary for the success of humanity. We must make eternity the primary and the most important thing in our lives when we are "in-time." Eternity trumps everything. We were in eternity before we came into our "in-time" experience, and we will return to a completely "in-eternity" experience when our spirit leaves our body. The "in-time" and "in-eternity" realities and their differences and their impact on humanity are not understood by most people. This knowledge and how it applies to our lives personally, and how all of this is a part of our Creator's plan for good for us, individually and collectively, is not being taught in school, at church nor in our homes. Humanity functions completely from an "in-time" perspective without consideration of our eternity. **This simple but profound understanding will change everything. How we function and how we conduct the living of our lives—when changed to reflect eternity—will produce desirable outcomes both now and in eternity. The results we are created to desire and which our spirits and minds long for are eternal.** This is important. This will change our lives for good. A new day of goodness and success will dawn for humanity and we will be better for it.

Hope cannot be replaced, and humanity requires hope. Hope is not optional. Humanity's desire for good and the expectation of that being accomplished and our belief and the confidence that the good we expect will be completed and fulfilled is the very substance of what our lives are about. While we know there is evil in our world, we must also know and believe that good always triumphs. Triumph may not appear as we have perceived it in our minds. That is why we have the privilege, the responsibility and the pleasure of learning how to determine and to define how our Creator describes the victory that is always present in the experiences we encounter in the living of our lives. This is why and how we must then begin the deliberate and the calculated programming of our mind, to agree with all that He says. He said that He would keep us in perfect peace if our minds stay on Him, and that would be because we trust Him. Confidence. Assurance. Victory.

Tragically, in 2012 on our planet more than eight hundred thousand individual people and fellow members of humanity chose to end their own lives. That number is staggering and overwhelming. Why? The most common reason given for their choice of action was because "they had no hope, they saw no way out of their situations, their circumstances and their relationships. No confidence, no belief and no expectation of improvement."

Life without hope is not life at all. It is merely existence. The burdens and the challenges of dealing with life without hope can often appear to become too much for us to bear. Our mind is a hard taskmaster. I am convinced this is where the battle is won or lost. It is my observation and personal belief that anyone who ends their own life has lost the battle in their mind and with their mind. Their mind has become in charge of their thoughts and the mind itself is directing their actions. It is their mind that is convincing them that there is no hope. The power of the mind is huge. Our mind rules our lives. If we do not take control of what we allow our mind to think, and consciously develop and deliberately manage our thoughts, the garbage and the lies from the Kingdom of Darkness that so flood our thoughts with lies continually will take root and lead us down the path of deception, to failure. It will direct us and lead us to our destruction and in many cases to our self-destruction. We must realize and be aware of the gravity and the overwhelming, complete seriousness of this reality in our mind. Our mind and our thoughts can terrorize us constantly. Without proper programming, our mind will rule us incorrectly and lead to our destruction. We must act wisely. We must realize that if we are not actively and proactively programming our mind and our thoughts to create our beliefs and our belief system, then someone else is. Our programming must be so that we are in agreement with what our Creator God says about everything: our thoughts about who we are, and where we go for our hope and for our help when we have need. We cannot allow someone else to program our mind and control the way we think and determine what we believe. **<u>It is what we believe that decides our actions</u>** — every time, without fail.

THIS IS NOT CASUAL, NOR IS IT SOMETHING THAT WE CAN TAKE LIGHTLY.

<u>Programming for our mind</u> –

"If your heart is broken, you'll find God right there. If you're kicked in the gut, he'll help you catch your breath. Disciples so often get into trouble; still, God is there every time. He's your bodyguard, shielding every bone; not even a finger gets broken."

Psalms 34:18–20 – The Message

"Lord, you know the hopes of the helpless; surely you will hear their cries and comfort them. You will bring justice to the orphans and the oppressed, so mere people can no longer terrify them."

Psalms 10:17 – New Living Translation

"A happy heart is good medicine and a cheerful <u>mind works healing</u>, but a broken spirit dries up the bones ."

Proverbs 17:22 – Amplified Bible

"Know too, that wisdom (facts apply / knowledge

applies to you personally) is good for your soul (mind). If you find it, your reward will be a bright future and an enduring hope."

Proverbs 24: 14 – The Voice.

"For I know the plans that I have for you," says the Eternal, "plans for peace, not evil, to give you a future and hope – never forget that. At that time you will call out for me, and I will hear. You will pray and I will listen. You will look for me intently, and you will find me. Yes, I will be found by you," says the Eternal.

Jeremiah 29:11, 12 – The Voice

"We were given this hope when we were saved. (if we already have something, we don't need to hope for it. But if we look forward to something we don't yet have, we must wait patiently and confidently.)"

Romans 8:24, 25 – New Living Translation

"Rejoice in our confident hope. Be patient in trouble, and keep on praying."

Romans 12:12 – New Living Translation

"And the Scriptures give us hope and encouragement as we wait patiently for God's promises to be fulfilled."

Romans 15:4b – New Living Translation

"So God gave us two unchanging things: His promise and His oath. These prove that it is impossible for God to lie. As a result, we who come to God for refuge might be encouraged to seize that hope that is set before us. That hope is real and true; an anchor to steady our restless souls (minds) a hope that leads us back to behind the curtain where God is;"

Hebrews 6:18–20a – The Voice

The above Scripture from Romans 15:4, states that "the Scriptures give us hope and encouragement as we wait patiently for God's promises to be fulfilled." It is tragic but true that the Scriptures have been hijacked by religion. Because of that, the Scriptures are viewed by many of humanity as a religious listing of "do's and don'ts." From that perspective they become primarily a tool for religious judgment and condemnation. The very thing that our Creator has provided to us for our hope and for our encouragement has become religious. The Scriptures are not religious. They are relational. Timothy said that "all Scripture is inspired by God and is useful to teach us what is true, and to make us realize what is wrong in our lives. It corrects us when we are wrong and teaches us to do what is right."

In the training of people who are in sales, we say that it is better to internalize knowledge about the product than to just memorize the material. To internalize means to make the information a part of one's nature by learning the material through the unconscious assimilation of the material. To memorize means to commit to memory. To internalize means to make the information you and who you are. An effective relationship with our Creator God is not made up of simply knowing about Him, going to church or being able to say Scriptures. Just saying Scriptures can become nothing more than words that we repeat. They must become a part of us.

Our Creator says that His Word is alive and that His Word is powerful. The Word has energy; the Word is moving. The Word is sharper than the sharpest double-edged sword. It cuts both ways. The Word separates and identifies for us the difference between mind/soul—thoughts, feelings, emotions and what is spirit—eternal. The Word allows humanity to analyze and judge the very thoughts and purposes of their heart/spirit.

Hebrews 4:12 – Personal Paraphrase

To even the most casual observer it is obvious that the aggregate of people living together in the community of humanity on planet Earth have lost hope. Over eight hundred thousand chose to end their own lives in 2012. Our culture has become a climate of despair. How did we get here? The prevailing trends of public opinion are not directed towards the development of hope. This is such a great tragedy for humanity. Actually, the opposite is true. There has never been a time on earth when the provision of hope for humanity has been greater. The evidence of hope is overwhelming. Hope is not the absence of struggle, nor is it a time when there is no opposition. Hope is the awareness of the plan that guarantees victory and success, and the understanding of how to get there—knowing what the outcome is from the beginning. There is no reason for fear or doubt. The available revelation of our Creator's complete provision for humanity's success is presented to each person thousands of times daily. His plan (the Kingdom System), along with the knowledge of how it works and how we engage the system in our personal lives for our benefit *(Kingdomnomics)*, through the dynamics of our choices of conduct and behavior, is increasing continually. We know and we understand how to deliver this system *(Kingdom Deployment)* into society to impact our culture through proper and correct thinking from the perspective of eternity. This is a great time to be alive. This is a time when we have great hope and we can see tremendous expectation. May we have eyes to see and ears to hear what the Spirit is saying to humanity.

> *"While our story may appear hopeless now, often later on we can look back on history (His Story!) And discover God's plan at work in our lives during that time ...* ***Hope is not wishful thinking, but trusting God Himself and what He has promised.****"* *Fred Brittner*

Summary and Conclusion

This is the third book in the three-book series about the Kingdom System. We began with the presentation of *The Kingdom System: A Pattern for Guaranteed Success*. The facts and their understanding about the existence of a plan for our success that is from our Creator God are outlined in the first book. In the second book in the series we provide an overview of Kingdomnomics, or the laws of the Kingdom System, titled *Kingdomnomics: The Dynamics of Conduct and Behavior*. We present these laws as more accurately being defined and described as dynamics of conduct and behavior, more than as laws of regulation and compliance. These dynamics are provided for all of humanity, as guidance or how-to directions for engaging the system into each of our lives. Understanding dynamics and their operation provides the instructions for making the system work for each of us individually and collectively as a people. In this book, and the last book in this three-book series about the Kingdom System, *Kingdom Deployment: Operating in Your Created Design for Your Eternal Purpose*, deployment is presented as the method that we use to deliver the Kingdom System. Kingdom

Deployment is the method that we use to introduce Kingdom Dynamics into society for positive impact on our culture in order to allow humanity to choose desirable Kingdom outcomes.

Why is it important that we know about the Kingdom System? Why is it important that we understand how the system works through the dynamics of conduct and behavior? Why is it important that we make Kingdom deployment our primary goal and purpose, and through our conscious, concentrated and deliberate efforts we choose to deliver this knowledge and this understanding to all of humanity?

Humanity has tried the systems of the world and they have all failed; government, economy, media, family, education, arts and entertainment, religion and all of their extensions do not provide the environment or the ingredients necessary for humanity to succeed in life. Success is not part of their design. Justice and equality cannot be found in the systems of the world. Frustration and hopelessness are epidemic. Humanity is desperate. When more than eight hundred thousand people choose to end their own lives in a single year on our planet, **we must act. We cannot allow the defeated Satan to deceive another person**.

The Kingdom System is the **correct choice to the alternative systems of the world**. Our Creator and our God would not leave humanity without a plan and without a system that works for their good, and a system that provides us with the purpose and the meaning that is necessary for the living of our lives. All of the systems of the Kingdom of Darkness are substitutes; they are phony and do not work. God Himself, as Jesus Christ, delivered the Kingdom System to the earth and

He taught humanity extensively about the Kingdom and how it functions when He was on earth. It was the primary message of His teachings while He was present on earth. When He departed, He then left His Word and His Spirit on earth so that humanity could learn and know how to experience all that the Kingdom is, and know how to fulfill the mandate that He charged, redeemed and restored humanity to demonstrate to others how they can live and experience a Kingdom-first life on our planet. The plan is present on the earth and is ready to be engaged in by all of humanity for the glory (reputation) of our God and for the good of all of humanity. It is the goodness of our God that draws humanity into a relationship with Him.

> ***Romans 2:4 (based on New Living Translation)***
> ***"Don't you see how wonderfully kind, tolerant, and patient God is with you? Does this mean nothing to you? Can't you see that his kindness is intended to turn you from your sin/transgression?" (And, to draw you into a right relationship with Him.)***
> ***Personal Paraphrase***

This is the **Good News.** How have so many of us been deceived for so long? It is not reasonable nor is it remotely conceivable that humanity would accept that the Creator, who provides so marvelously and so magnificently for everything that we could possibly think or possibly imagine, would not provide a good plan for the living of our lives. His provisions are so wonderful that we cannot imagine them. A Creator/God who is like that **would absolutely provide** a plan for our success and for our successful living on our planet. Can we believe that the best He offers for our lives would be for us to experience one defeat after another by His defeated enemy? The enemy who wants to be king! The one whom He has defeated. The one whose power and the keys he had to the Kingdom of the earth, that He. He has taken away from him. This is not reasonable. The Creator of all things has an excellent plan. His plans for us are for good, for hope and for a future of prosperity and good health. We must know the truth and reject all the lies of the defeated Satan.

Many times, believers say, "God knows my need and He will take care of it." He has taken care of it. God does not respond to need without our planting a seed, our seed. Our system of faith is an interactive system involving competing or conflicting forces. We must act. We must make the choice to walk by faith and to practice faith. Our faith is built and established on the Word of our God. We must program our mind to agree with His Word. We cannot be fooled by the things that we see with our mortal eyes. We must know for certain that our faith is the assurance of things we have hoped for (or what we are hoping for), with the absolute conviction that they are realities we have not yet seen.

We are overcomers. In every situation we are made to triumph and to experience victory through Christ Jesus. No weapon formed against us will prosper. When our enemy comes at us from one direction, our God will send him scattering in seven directions. If our enemy persists, our God will destroy them before our very eyes. A thousand may fall at our side and ten thousand at our right hand but it will not come near us. We have been provided a shield of faith that we can use to deflect every fiery dart from the defeated Satan. Greater is He who is living in and working through us than he that is in the world.

We must allow eternity to be who we are, what we are and what we choose to do. No matter how much effort it takes to program ourselves so that eternity and eternal considerations become our first and primary consideration, **we must do just that**. Learning to think eternally will change everything. It is only when our enemy, the defeated Satan, can deceive humanity into an **"in-time" only** consideration for our thoughts, actions and desires, that we make unwise choices with real, unpleasant consequences "in-time" and for our eternity. The most important relationships for humanity when we are "in-time" are the things that are eternal. Our "in-time" experience is only a nanosecond in our eternity. That nanosecond is important, extremely important. It is during that brief period of our eternity that we choose and decide what our life experience for all of our eternity will be. This does not begin just when we die. We are in our eternity now, right now on planet Earth. When our eternal spirit leaves our earthly body / tabernacle / tent / soma, it is too late. We cannot change what we have decided that our eternity will be. While our present body has breath/life, this is the time when we are given the privilege, the opportunity and the responsibility of deciding what our eternal experience is to be.

The choices are not difficult. There are only two. Will we choose eternal life now, while we are living in the "in-time" portion of our eternity? We can begin to experience the relationship of a reborn, recreated spirit that fellowships and communicates directly with our Creator/God. Or will we choose eternal damnation and be separated from God forever, during all of our eternity? This does not just begin when our body dies and our spirit leaves its earth suit. This choice separates us from our God now, and this choice continues that separation for all of our eternity. This is not a difficult choice when we know and when we understand eternity and when we know the facts. It is only when we do not consider eternity—as if it does not exist—and when we choose to make our decisions and choices based on our "in-time" and present position only.

Life on planet Earth is meant to be the period "in-time" when we develop, when we design and when we build our eternal relationship with our Creator. The defeated Satan seems to have gotten humanity off course concerning relationship. We concentrate on the things that are temporary and we often ignore the things that are eternal. It appears that religion has hijacked relationship and substituted religious regulations and compliance, which do not require relationship. We only have to follow the rules and stay within the parameters. There is no relationship required. Our God is not a religious God. When our God was on earth, it was the religious people who had difficulties with Him. Their challenge was mostly because He was not religious and because He was and is relational. "Why are you hanging out with them? That is not whom you should be seen with. Why do you meet their needs, heal their diseases, straighten their limbs, et cetera? Why do you perform these miracles on the wrong day of the week?! This is against our religious teachings, our religious customs and our religious traditions." Relationship is how our Creator God's fellowship with humanity began. In the garden there were no written laws. Communication and direction from God were given directly, firsthand and in person through fellowship, through spending time together. God is the God of relationship.

> ***Relationship requires fellowship.***
> ***Fellowship requires that we spend time together.***
> ***Spending time together requires that we give the time.***

We are told to seek after the Kingdom with all of our might. To be ravenously hungry for the Kingdom and to make our pursuit of the Kingdom System of our God the number one priority in our life. We are told that the Kingdom is eternal, it is everlasting and it will never end. We are told it will smash all of the other systems on our planet into nothingness. The Kingdom System and everything about the Kingdom is eternal. **If it is not eternal, it is not Kingdom.** We are also told that when we make the eternal things of the eternal Kingdom first in our lives and the primary objective of our pursuit, all the temporal things that humanity desires will come to us naturally.

We must thoroughly do the research and discover for ourselves how much time we invest in the process of developing our eternal relationship. The relationship that is eternal with our eternal God can only be developed through the time we spend together in fellowship with Him. Normally we spend more than twenty years of our "in-time" lives developing our minds in the pursuit of an education for a chosen field of employment. How much time do we spend fellowshipping with our God to develop our spirit, to hear and to know our Creator God and to recognize His voice? Has God called us to employment or to deployment? Should our priority be our income or our outcome?

Is all of this important to our God? Does employment or deployment, income or outcome matter at all to Him? Is He hoping we will make some good decisions so that He can adjust everything and make everything turn out all right? Does our God have a prewritten plan and a purpose for our eternity that is established for each of us before we are even born? Is it reasonable to believe that everything is haphazard and "what will be, will be"? It is up to us to work it all out and make something happen.

In the letter to the Romans that the Holy Spirit God inspired Paul to write, He discussed plan, purpose, created design and eternal purpose.

> ***Romans 8:28 (based on Amplified Translation)***
> ***"We are assured and we know that our God being a partner in their/our labor) that all things work together and are (fitting into a plan) a plan that is good to us, and a plan that is good for us as, those who love God and those who are called according to (His) created design and for His/their eternal purpose."***
> ***(Personal Paraphrase)***

We are told that every day of our lives is written in His book before our first day begins. Every moment was laid out. We are told that no matter where we go, His plans and His will follow us. He is wherever we are, and He is there for the purpose of protecting us, guiding and directing us and for assisting us with the plans that He has uniquely, specifically and creatively designed for each of us. We are told that His **prewritten** plans are plans that are for good for us, plans that are for hope for each of us. The plans are for a clear and bright future of prosperity and good health. He states clearly that His plans for us do not include disaster.

So what is the difficulty? Where is the disconnect? Why so often are our life experiences filled with challenges and the challenges often appear to end up as catastrophic disasters? Zig Ziglar enjoyed saying that "you cannot hit a target that you cannot see." I can speak best from my personal experience. I simply did not know that there is another choice and that this choice is completely from our Creator/God. There is no human influence or human origin in this provision. This is not an alternative or substitute for anything. This is the original choice, and this choice is the provision that comes to us solely from our Creator God. **This is the correct choice to the alternative systems of the world**. This choice is the system provided for us so that we can engage in it and understand the related dynamics of the system in order to change and direct our lives to desirable Kingdom outcomes. This system will positively impact our life experiences and produce outcomes that are different than the outcomes we are experiencing from the systems of the world. This system will provide good outcomes for us in the living of our lives. We mistakenly believe what we are experiencing is the only choice we have. Life is busy. We become so busy that we do not believe we have the time or the available energy to address anything that is possibly different. We feel compelled to continue on as we are in order to complete the task at hand. We concentrate on living our lives, and try desperately to make the knowledge and the understanding that we presently have work for us as best we can. A familiar saying that seems appropriate here is: that "When you are up to your neck in alligators, it is difficult to remember that you went there to drain the pond." Adding to our propensity to resist change is the fact that too often we have tried other dynamics and they have not worked.

As we stated in *The Kingdom System,* our mind contains the data that we have installed there. This is where we have stored the facts as we know them. Our mind is the source from which we retrieve what may be correctly defined as our knowledge. This forms our vantage point and decides the position from which all of our understanding is viewed and interpreted.

We must recognize the strategies and the deceits of the defeated Satan and put a stop to them by speaking our God's Word out of our mouth in faith. **We must act.** "If we continue to do what we have been doing, we will continue to get what we have been getting." The Great Book of Learning is replete with encouragement for humanity to continue to learn and to view learning as a lifelong experience. At no time during the "in-time" portion of our eternity is there any hint of the suggestion that we will or should ever cease to learn. Learning about a subject is often called the discipline of the particular subject. In the Great Book of Learning, there are real consequences described for those who hate the discipline of learning. The dynamic of being teachable has a huge impact on the quality of life and the life experiences for humanity, both in the outcomes that our choices select for us, and in the experiences of the living of our life itself. We must be capable of being taught, and we must be willing to learn. We must be proactive. We are told to go after learning with all of our might, with everything that is within us. Our passion for learning is described as being "ravenously hungry" for learning. This does not describe a nonchalant, lackadaisical, laissez-faire approach, but rather an intense passion that burns with a flaming desire to accomplish and to achieve success in the subject area of learning.

Learning always creates change. Learning and change go together; they are partners. Humanity is naturally inclined to resist change. Learning and change can bring with them a certain amount of discomfort. I believe that is because we have a fear of the unknown. As a young officer in my early twenties, I recall receiving orders for Vietnam in the late 1960s. I recall imagining what I would face upon arrival and what Vietnam would be like. There were accounts on television and in the newspapers, showing images of the airport in Saigon being rocketed and stating that people were killed. I wondered if upon arrival we would have to unload quickly and run to bunkers or somewhere else that was safe. Our arrival was uneventful. The arrival was no different than if we had landed in Atlanta or New York City. Because this was my first time to visit Vietnam and because I did not know what to expect, my imagination was working overtime. I was prepared for whatever we encountered. On return trips to Vietnam my imagination did not have the freedom to create such pictures in my mind. I had knowledge and experience that I did not have before.

We cannot remain where we are. We can no longer sit quietly by and passively observe as humanity and our planet are being destroyed by the lies and the deceits of the Kingdom of Darkness.

Humanity is being deceived and our societies have become so deeply ingrained in the systems of the world that there appears to be no knowledge or recognition of the systems of our God. All of the systems of the world lead to bondage and destruction, often self-destruction. The systems of the world operate by tyranny and oppression. They come with overwhelming and overbearing chains of slavery for those who believe in their lies and for those who choose to follow them. Not a single system of the world system operates for the good of humanity. Even a casual observer can recognize that the motives and the outcomes of the systems of the world are not for the good of humanity. Thank God there is another choice, and this choice is <u>the correct choice to the alternative systems of the world.</u>

Government, economy, media, family, education, arts and entertainment, religion and their many extensions do not have humanity and the well-being of humanity as their primary goal, as they should. Each sphere of influence is more concerned about their preservation than their interest in being a service and a benefit to their citizens or their subjects. The specific acts and the chosen practices of each of these cultural centers are clearly to enhance their own power, to increase their personal wealth and to solidify their control over humanity. They do this by exaggerating their own importance, by misrepresenting their history and by distorting their reputation.

When do we decide that enough is enough? How long will we continue to refuse to change? When will we take a stand? When will we acknowledge that for there to be relevant and effectual change, the change must begin with us? <u>**We must change**</u>.

When will we speak the truth and denounce the lies? When will those in government stand up and say, "No, this is not good for our citizens. It is not right for us to pass laws that we impose on our citizens and we then exempt ourselves. This is deceptive." When will bankers stand up and say, "No, this is not right. We have more disposable money now than we have ever had. We will pay a decent return on your money and we will provide funding with reasonable requirements and at a reasonable cost." When will attorneys say, "No, I will not take this case. It may be legal, but it is not right. I will not pursue opportunities just because I know that the insurance companies and those with assets will pay rather than face the expense and the uncertainty of a skewed trial." When will media not concentrate on sensationalism and present facts without opinion? When will moviemakers promote honorable values and virtues, and refuse to support and promote extramarital sex, homosexuality and abortion? Why is it necessary to see multiple and repeated murders over and over again? Why is it necessary to see so many substitute examples of a real family? Why do art and entertainment have to be vulgar and common and void of true beauty and character? When did effective religion become the size of the facility and the number who are attending? Why does our education exclude the source of all knowledge, and deny our true standard for dignity and for fairness, for equality and for justice? When will we say no, you and I? When will we have had enough? When will we become active and engaged in the process of sharing truth and restoring the foundations of our faith?

The famous quote by Edmund Burke correctly says that "The

only thing necessary for the triumph of evil is for good men to do nothing."

So what do we do? Do we protest? Do we march, riot, turn over and burn cars, destroy private property and violate the laws that are there to protect everyone and their property? I am convinced that <u>there is never a good reason to do wrong.</u> The standard for all conduct and behavior by humanity must be:

1) <u>Do what is right.</u> What has been deemed to be legal by the systems of the world may be different from what our Creator God says to us. He has outlined what is acceptable conduct and behavior within the Kingdom Government System of our God. The courts and the judges of this world may make decisions and declare rulings that do not agree with our God. One day even the Supreme Court Justices of the United States will stand before the real supreme court of Heaven and will answer for their actions to the one who is the one and the only true Justice forever. We must follow the legislature of Heaven.

2) <u>Love mercy.</u> Do not take advantage of others just because you can. When someone does wrong, whether they make a mistake or if they intentionally make the choice to do wrong, we must be merciful. That does not mean to excuse their behavior, but to understand that we must extend mercy in order to receive mercy. Having mercy is the correct thing to do. Acts of cruelty and selfishness cannot be excused, nor can they be tolerated. To correct such actions we must act within the guidelines contained in the Great Book of Learning.

3) <u>Walk humbly before our God.</u> We cannot be puffed up and overly proud of ourselves because of the favor and the blessings that we have received. We cannot beat ourselves on our chest and declare how special we are. We must always be aware that it is by the grace of God that we are who we are. It is only that grace which separates us from others who are without the relationship of Christ. We can never look down on others less fortunate or those who have not yet heard the Good News of the Gospel. Our blessings must be captured in a way that can be converted to energy and activity that will show and will declare the goodness of our God. With thankful hearts we must welcome all of our brothers and sisters from every race, kindred and tongue, into our fellowship.

What is it that all of humanity everywhere is looking for? What do they want to see, to know and to understand? They are searching for truth, justice and equality. Truth that will make a difference in the experiences of the living of their lives. Truth that will allow them to influence and to direct the outcomes of their lives to good outcomes. Humanity is desperate. All of the substitutes fail. The Great Book of Learning, the Manufacturer's Handbook, tells us that nothing under the sun will satisfy humanity except the personal knowledge and a personal relationship with the Creator God. I have experienced this search firsthand. I have found something that works for me and for others with whom I am able to share my findings.

The results of my search, along with the corresponding findings, are presented in the Kingdom System Series trilogy.

1) The Kingdom System: A Pattern for Guaranteed Success

These are the facts about the plan and the plan's existence, the system that was delivered to the earth by our God Himself in the person of Jesus Christ. This knowledge provides direction for humanity and supplies the meaning and the purpose for our dysfunctional lives. When we do not have this knowledge and when we attempt to live successful lives in our own power and in our own ability, we experience frustration and defeat. These facts are the **knowledge** that we need in order to live successful lives on earth.

2) Kingdomnomics: The Dynamics of Conduct and Behavior

The system operates by dynamics. Dynamics are best described and defined as an interactive system of competing and/or conflicting forces. This is to demonstrate how we engage in the system. This shows how we become a part of the system and how we make the system become a part of us. This is how we convert the **knowledge** that we have learned into personal **wisdom** for us. This is how we make the knowledge personal and effective as applied **wisdom** for us.

3) Kingdom Deployment: Operating in Your Created Design for Your Eternal Purpose

In this book we address how our personal knowledge and wisdom of the Kingdom System and the related dynamics fit into our Creator's plan for all of humanity. We determine the role that we play in His plan. All that our Creator does in our lives is always completely about us, the individual. His concern is also always about and for all of humanity. There is always an individual and a corporate application to our Creator and our God's plans and actions.

In this research there were several new approaches to familiar subjects. We considered employment versus deployment, and income versus outcome. The entire understanding and the application of eternity into the lives are fresh and revolutionary. This understanding will change our lives and our life experiences for good, betterment for us and for humanity. We determined that for each of us, everyone who ever graces planet Earth, there is a specific and unique plan. That plan is creatively designed for their eternal purpose by our Creator God before they are ever conceived, eternally. How they arrived on earth does not change this.

Much research has gone into the information that is presented. Primarily, the Great Book of Learning provided the principal thought, but many authors and teachers and their works were considered. There is much wonderful material available. What evolved was completely different than anything I had read or heard. Where the core values and the understanding were consistent and constant, the presentation, the vantage points, the approach, the application and the results are different.

What is presented here is neither theory nor speculative thought for consideration. Our family has walked this out, and we have found it accurate and effective. Many with whom we have shared these truths have achieved similar results. Our prayers and our belief for you is that this will empower you to experience the relationship of success that our God has planned and has provided for you.

May our God's richest blessings always be yours.

Positional and Declaration Statements

In our learning research, we have seen the necessity and the power of the spoken Word. In the process of developing and programming our mind to think like our God thinks, we have determined that just thinking something will not accomplish the desired change or results. When we believe in our spirit, we must confess with our mouth that belief before it becomes effective and active. When our God functioned creatively, He activated His thoughts by speaking from His mouth. The power of life creatively is in the tongue. We create our reality by speaking our belief that is based on the Words of our God, out loud from our mouth.

In each book there are provided sayings that reflect what the Word of our God says in common language. Our family has used these and similar sayings for many years. They are a source of strength and reassurance. We offer them for your personal use. Please modify them as the Holy Spirit God so directs you as you use them.

Deuteronomy 28

Father, in the name of Jesus, the Charlie and Fran Lewis family, our heirs and our descendants forever, declare that we obey Your Word and that we keep Your Commands. Father, You set us high above all the nations of the world. We experience all of Your blessings continually and lavishly.

We are blessed in the city. We are blessed in the country. Everywhere that we go we are blessed. We are blessed in the fields of labor (all of the work of our hands) that You have given to us. Our children are blessed (our birth children / our spiritual and our business children). Our crops are blessed (all of the business and industry) and produce exponentially. Our herds and our flocks are blessed (the companies, the individuals and the groups with whom we work). Our fruit baskets are full and our bread bowls overflow. (We have neither lack nor deficiency of provision). We bring to You the first fruits of all of our labors, Father, because they belong to You, our God. We walk under the open windows of Heaven. You pour out blessings greater than we can contain. We share the blessings that we receive with those around us who are in need. We do so under the direction of the Holy Spirit God.

We are blessed wherever we go, wherever we come from and everywhere that our names are mentioned.

We are the largest contributors in the world to the spreading of the Good News of the Gospel of the Kingdom of our God. Billions of men and women and boys and girls are freed from the tyranny and the oppression and the chains of slavery from the Kingdom of Darkness that have them bound, and they come into right relationship with You, our God, and You become their God.

When our enemies attack us from one direction, You send them scattering in seven directions. If they persist, You destroy them before our very eyes. A thousand may fall at our side and ten thousand may fall at our right hand, but it will not come near us.

Lord, You guarantee blessings on everything that we do, and You fill our storehouses with grain (from abundant, lavish harvests). You bless us, O Lord, in the lands that You have given to us.

Lord, we obey Your commands and we walk in Your ways. You establish us as Your holy people, Lord, and all the nations of the world see that we are a people claimed by the Lord, and they stand in awe of You, our God.

Lord, You bless us with prosperity in the lands You have given to us (spiritually, mentally, physically —our health, Lord—emotionally, relationally and financially). You bless us with many children

(naturally and spiritually), numerous livestock (those who produce for the labors that You have given to us) and abundant crops (we harvest an abundant, lavish return). Lord, You send rain (moisture/ nourishment) at the proper time (when it is needed) from Your rich treasury in the heavens, and You bless all the work that we do. Father, we lend to many nations, but we never ever need to borrow from them. We listen to the commands of the Lord and we are careful to obey You.

You make us the head and not the tail; we are above and not beneath. We crush the defeated Satan's head with our heel. Greater are You, Lord God, who is living in and working through us, than he that is in this present evil world.

Positional: Change Your Environment

• Father God, in the name that is above all names, Jesus, the Charlie and Fran Lewis family, our heirs and our descendants forever declare that You, as the Lord Jesus Christ, are Lord over our spirits, our minds and our bodies. (Philippians 2:9–11)

• Jesus, You are made unto us to be wisdom, righteousness, sanctification, redemption and the full restoration of the Kingdom System of our God in our lives, both in relationship and in practical benefit. We can and we do all things through You. Lord Jesus, You are our strength. (1 Corinthians 1:30; Philippians 4:13)

• Lord, You are our shepherd, we do not want. You, Father God, supply all our needs according to Your riches in glory in Christ Jesus. Your glory is all around us, and we reach out into the invisible Kingdom and pull into us all that we need in the visible Kingdom. (Psalm 23; Philippians 4:19)

• We have the mind of Christ Jesus. We hold the thoughts, the feelings and the purposes of Your Spirit and of Your Mind (1 Corinthians 2:16). We are believers and not doubters. We hold fast to our confession of faith. We decide to walk by faith and

to practice faith. Our faith comes from hearing Your Word, Lord Jesus. Jesus, You are the author and the developer of our faith. (Hebrews 4:14; 11:6; 12:2; Romans 10:17)

• Your love, Father God, has been poured out in our Spirits and into our minds by the Holy Spirit God, and Your love dwells in us continually and richly. We keep ourselves in the Kingdom of Light, in Your love and in Your Word, and the wicked one touches us not. (Romans 5:5; 1 John 4:6)

• We tread upon serpents and scorpions and over all of the power of the enemy. We take our shield of faith, and we quench every fiery dart of the defeated Satan. Greater are You, Lord God, who is living in and who is working through us than he who is in the world. (Psalm 91:13; Ephesians 6:16; 1 John 4:4, 5:18)

• We are delivered from this present evil world. We are seated with You, Christ Jesus, in heavenly places. We reside in the Kingdom of God's dear Son. The law of the Spirit of Life in Christ Jesus has made us free from the law of sin and death. (Galatians 1:4; Ephesians 2:6; Colossians 1:13; Romans 8:2)

• We do not fear, because You, Father God, have given us the spirit of power and Your love, and we operate from a sound mind. God, You are on our side. (2 Timothy 1:7; Romans 8:31)

- **We hear and we recognize the voice of the Good Shepherd. We hear and we know our Father's voice, and the voice of a stranger we will not follow. We roll our works upon You, Lord Jesus. We commit and we trust them completely to You. You cause our thoughts to become agreeable with Your will, and so are our plans established and our plans succeed. (John 10:27; Proverbs 16:3)**

- **We are world overcomers, Father God, because we are born of You. We represent the Father and Jesus' will. We are useful members of the Body of Christ. We are Your workmanship, Father God, recreated in Christ Jesus. You, Father God, are continually and effectively at work in us to lead us to both want to do and then to do Your good pleasure. (1 John 5:4–5; Ephesians 2:10; Philippians 2:13)**

- **We let Your Word dwell in us richly. You have begun a good work in us and You will continue until the day of Your appearing.**

Praise be to Your name, our Father. You are always faithful.

Prayer of Commitment to the Word

Father, in the name of Jesus, the Charlie and Fran Lewis family, our heirs and our descendants forever, declare that we commit ourselves to walk in Your Word. We recognize that Your Word is integrity itself. Your Word is steadfast. Your Word is sure. Your Word is eternal. We trust our lives to the provisions of Your Word.

You have sent Your Word forth into our spirit and into our mind. We let Your Word dwell in us richly in all wisdom. Your Word does not depart out of our mouth. Your Word is all that we speak. We meditate in Your Word day and night so that we may diligently act upon Your Word. Your Word is the incorruptible seed that is abiding and living in our spirit and in our mind. Your Word is growing mightily in us now; Your Word is becoming dominant and produces Your nature and Your life.

We thank You, Father, that Your Word is our counsel—Your Word gives us insight and direction; Your Word is our shield—Your Word forms a hedge of protection around us that the defeated Satan cannot penetrate; Your Word is our buckler—Your Word keeps us upright and connected to You; You are our complete source

and our complete supply; Your Word is our powerful weapon in battle that always gives us victory. Your Word is the lamp unto our feet and the light unto our path. Your Word makes our way straight before us, and we never ever stumble or fall because our steps are ordered by Your Word. We recognize the strategies and the deceits of the defeated Satan, and we put a stop to them by speaking Your Word out of our mouth in faith.

We are confident, Father, that You and Your perfect plan for our lives are at work in us, to lead us to both want to do and then to do Your good pleasure. We exalt Your Word. We hold Your Word in the highest esteem. We give Your Word first place in our lives. We boldly and we confidently declare that our spirit and our mind are fixed upon You and established on the solid foundation of the living Word of God.

Amen.

Appendix

Foundational Statement

1. Lewis, Charlie. *The Kingdom System: A Pattern for Guaranteed Success,* Kingdom Media, LLC, 2014 by Charlie Lewis
2. Lewis, Charlie. *Kingdomnomics: The Dynamics of Conduct and Behavior,* Kingdom Media, LLC, 2014 by Charlie Lewis

Introduction

1. Lewis, Charlie. *The Kingdom System: A Pattern for Guaranteed Success,* Kingdom Media, LLC, 2014 by Charlie Lewis
2. Lewis, Charlie. *Kingdomnomics: The Dynamics of Conduct and Behavior,* Kingdom Media, LLC, 2014 by Charlie Lewis

Chapter 1

1. Proverbs 2:2–12 (New Living Translation)

Chapter 2

1. Mark 10:30 (King James Version)
2. Luke 23:46 (New Living Translation)
3. Acts 7:59 (New Living Translation)
4. Corinthians 5:1 (New Living Translation)
5. Genesis 21:33 (New Living Translation)
6. Deuteronomy 33:27 (New Living Translation)

7. Isaiah 26:4, 43:13, 40:8, 9:7 (New Living Translation)
8. Romans 9:5 (New Living Translation)
9. John 5:20, 12:25 (New Living Translation)
10. Daniel 7:14 (New Living Translation)
11. Peter 1:11, 1:25 (New Living Translation)
12. Daniel 2:44, 7:14, 4:34 (New Living Translation)
13. Psalms 119:89 (New International Version)
14. Psalm 136, 1–5 (New Living Translation)
15. Jeremiah 31:3 (New Living Translation)
16. Psalm 103:17, 100:5, 118:1 (King James Version)
17. Corinthians 4:18 (King James Version)
18. Timonthy 6:19 (King James Version)
19. Revelation 14:6 (New Living Translation)

Chapter 3

1. Romans 12:2 (Amplified), (New Living Translation)
2. Ephesians 5:26 (Amplified), (New Living Translation)

Chapter 4

1. Jeremiah 1:5 (New Living Translation), (Young's Literal Translation)
2. Galatians 1:15 (New Living Translation)
3. Psalms 139:15, 16 (New Living Translation)
4. Genesis 18:10 – Isaac – (Genesis 21:3)
5. Judges 13:3 – Samson – (Judges 13:24)

Chapter 5

1. Revelation 2:26 (Amplified Bible)

Chapter 6

1. Matthew 25:46 (New Living Translation)
2. Acton, Lord. http://www.brainyquote.com/quotes/authors/l/lord_acton.html
3. Adams, John. http://www.brainyquote.com/quotes/quotes/j/johnadams389106.html
4. www.nationaldebtclocks.org – *debt of our nations in our world.*
5. Zacharias, Ravi. http://www.goodreads.com/author/quotes/3577.Ravi_Zacharias
6. Keller, Helen. *"Fidelity"*
7. Giraudoux, Jean. *"Fidelity"*
8. Key, Ellen. *"Fidelity"*
9. Horace. *"Fidelity"*
10. Buckley, James L. *"Fidelity"*
11. Prager, Dennis. *" Integrity"*
12. Marley, Bob. *" Integrity"*
13. Brown, H. Jackson. *" Integrity"*
14. Eisenhower, Dwight D. *" Integrity"*
15. Winfrey, Oprah. *" Integrity"*
16. Ziglar, Zig. *" Integrity"*
17. Stanley, Charles. *" Integrity"*

18. Kravis, Henry. " *Integrity*"
19. Churchill, Winston. *"Morality"*
20. Zacharias, Ravi. *"Morality"*
21. Gandhi, Mahatma. *"Morality"*
22. Washington, George. *"Morality"*
23. Clarke, Arthur C. *"Morality"*
24. Schopenhauer, Arthur. *"Morality"*
25. Pauling, Linus. *"Morality"*
26. Gandhi, Mahatma. *"Morality"*
27. Crowley, Aleister. *"Morality"*
28. Thoreau, Henry David. *"Morality"*
29. Aristotle. *"Honor"*
30. Churchill, Winston. *"Honor"*
31. Roosevelt, Franklin D. *"Honor"*
32. Coolidge, Calvin. *"Honor"*
33. Socrates, *"Honor"*
34. Ingersoll, Robert Green. *"Honor"*
35. MacArthur, Douglas. *"Honor"*
36. Smiles, Samuel. *"Honor"*
37. Banks, Lloyd. *"Honor"*
38. Branch, Rickey. *"Honor"*

Chapter 7

1. Alcohol Use in the United States. www.niaaa.nih.gov
2. Proverbs 20:1 *(The Message)*
3. Proverbs 20:1 *(New Living Translation)*

Chapter 8

1. Proverbs 13:12 *(New Living Translation), (The Message)*
2. Psalm 25:5, 25:21, 31:24, 33:20, 33:22, 52:9, 62:5, 71:14, 119:114, 130:5
3. Munroe, Dr. Myles. "Our challenge in life is not who we are, but who we believe that we are."
4. Psalms 34:18–20 *(The Message)*
5. Psalms 10:17 *(New Living Translation)*
6. Proverbs 17:22 *(Amplified Bible)*
7. Proverbs 24:14 *(The Voice)*
8. Jeremiah 29:11, 12 *(The Voice)*
9. Romans 8:24, 25 *(New Living Translation)*
10. Romans 15:4b *(New Living Translation)*
11. Hebrews 6:18, 20a *(The Voice)*
12. Brittner, Fred. *"While our story may appear hopeless now, often later on we can look back on history (His Story!) And discover God's plan at work in our lives during that time … Hope is not wishful thinking, but trusting God Himself and what He has promised."*

Summary and Conclusion

1. Ziglar, Zig. "You cannot hit a target that you cannot see."
2. Burke, Edmund. "The only thing necessary for evil to triumph is for good men to do nothing."

All books are available at www.amazon.com

Kingdom Series

Volumen I

Volumen II

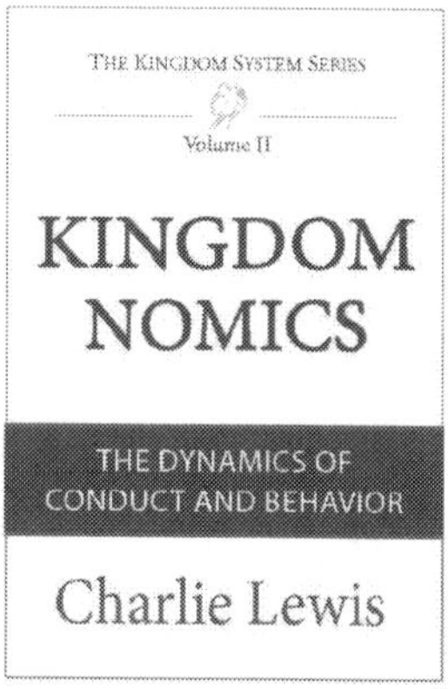

Volumen III

Also available in Spanish, Russian